THE TOP 100
Women
OF THE
Bible

THE TOP 100
Women
OF THE
Bible

Who They Are and *What* They Mean to You Today

PAMELA L. McQUADE

BARBOUR
PUBLISHING

ISBN 978-1-61626-249-5

Published by Barbour Publishing, Inc., P.O. Box 719, Uhrichsville, Ohio 44683, www.barbourbooks.com

Our mission is to publish and distribute inspirational products offering exceptional value and biblical encouragement to the masses.

Printed in the United States of America.

CONTENTS

INTRODUCTION

Read some Bible commentaries and you may see only minor references to events involving women. But the prophetesses, wives, sisters, and mothers of the Bible are strong, active, and often powerfully faithful. These people made a difference in the world, and without them, how much smaller our faith—and the biblical record—would be.

Read the scriptures, and you'll find women portrayed in politics and in the home, in the temple and in the workplace. No corner of human activity goes unreported by the Word. And nowhere does God denigrate women or their importance to the spread of the gospel. Indeed, women are honored and blessed for their faithfulness to God.

In this book, *The Top 100 Women of the Bible*, you'll find women of all sorts. Some are strong and faith filled, others are weak or wicked. A handful hold positions of worldly importance, while others—simple peasants, really—have changed the world even more than their seemingly more powerful sisters. In these stories you'll admire one woman's faith, while wondering what another was thinking in the path she pursued. But each woman inspires, warns, or leads us. And her example can turn us away from sin or draw us closer to God.

As you read, draw from the lives of these women. Learn from them how to live faithfully in a fallen world. And, as you turn to the scriptures that describe them, delight also in the Bible that brings them to you. For there, lived out before your eyes and placed in your hands to read again and again, is a record of what it means to be a faithful Christian.

God has a special place in His heart for women, as you'll discover from the ones that fill the pages of His Book.

ABIGAIL

His name was Nabal and his wife's name was Abigail.
She was an intelligent and beautiful woman,
but her husband, a Calebite,
was surly and mean in his dealings.

1 Samuel 25:3

Here is one of the Bible's great mismatched couples. Since it was the custom of the day to arrange marriages, Abigail had probably been wed to Nabal for his wealth, not for any meeting of the hearts. While she was a faithful and savvy woman, he was not only named "Fool" (the meaning of *Nabal*), his actions showed he was one.

Though women of that day generally had much less respect and authority than men, the Bible speaks highly of Abigail while recording only the mean-spiritedness and wrong-headedness of her husband. The two were certainly spiritually incompatible. While Abigail had faith, her husband had no time for God—certainly his attitudes and actions were not those of a faithful believer. Still, though theirs could not have been an easy relationship, resentment didn't crush Abigail's spirit. Instead, she used her many personal gifts and graces to bring the best to her household.

At the festive sheep-shearing time, the surly and greedy Nabal intentionally offended King David. Recognizing the danger, one of the wealthy landowner's servants knew whom to approach: He reported the situation to Nabal's wise wife. Immediately, Abigail understood the foolishness of turning down a polite request for support from the displaced David. Though the newly anointed king was fighting Saul for the throne, his warriors had protected Nabal's fields and clearly deserved some recompense. Food for his band of men did not seem an unreasonable request. Nabal had much, and the common custom of the day would have demanded that he share with those who had protected him and his household from harm.

Instead of wasting time arguing with her husband, Abigail prepared food for David's men and set off to approach their leader to make peace. She mounted her donkey not a moment too soon. On the road to David's camp, she met the warrior-king and his men, headed in her direction and intent on exacting retribution.

Abigail knew her husband's attitude had risked all his holdings and placed her in a difficult position—yet her dependence lay not on her spouse, but with God. Understanding that David was doing God's work and required her support, she provided it. That simple intervention and her humble words and attitude before Israel's anointed-but-on-the-run king prevented unnecessary bloodshed.

David immediately appreciated Abigail's faith and good qualities and praised God for her quick actions. If Nabal did not know how to recognize his wife's value, the king did. He turned aside his wrath because of this faithful woman's generous response.

While Abigail worked out a peace plan, her husband

partied. She returned to find him drunk, so not until the next day did she explain how she'd spent her day. Hearing what his wife had done, the brutish Nabal literally had a fit—perhaps experiencing a stroke. A few days later, he died.

David saw Nabal's death as God's justice and immediately sought Abigail's hand in marriage. In a moment, faithful Abigail moved from a fool's wife to a king's bride.

In Abigail we see many examples of faithfulness. When difficult relationships become part of our lives, we can follow her example. Will bitterness and resentment overwhelm our faith? Or, like her, can we trust God will make use even of our hardest situations? Do we do the good that falls our way, knowing that God's wisdom will bring benefit to ourselves and others?

Though matched with an unbelieving spouse, Abigail remained faithful to her Lord. Like her, do we resist allowing unsatisfactory relationships to stall us out in our faith and continue on, trusting our God?

Humility clothed Abigail's strength. No radical, angry woman, she paved the way for all women of strength to walk humbly before their God and make peace in broken relationships. God alone brings tranquility to broken lives. Abigail experienced that, and so can we. And, like Abigail, we may find that when we've passed through the troubles, God gives us a better life than we ever expected.

ABIHAIL

Rehoboam married Mahalath,
who was the daughter of David's son Jerimoth
and of Abihail, the daughter of Jesse's son Eliab.
2 CHRONICLES 11:18

Abihail, whose name means "father is strength," was the daughter of Jesse's first son Eliab, which means "God is father." She certainly had an impressive lineage, since her uncle David and his son Solomon became Israel's greatest kings. And Abihail married one of David's sons, possibly by a concubine.

Abihail's daughter Mahalath married a king, Rehoboam. But this mother's heart must have been saddened to watch the kingdom fall apart in her son-in-law's hands. Doubtless Mahalath also suffered as his wife, since Rehoboam had eighteen wives and sixty concubines. It couldn't have been a satisfying marriage.

Abihail proves that even a "premier family" background can't guarantee a trouble-free life. The Bible doesn't describe her sorrows, but we may easily read between the lines and understand that lineage isn't everything.

Today, it still doesn't matter if you hail from a family of great stature or a very humble one—troubles will come your way. Only God, the strongest Father, can protect His children and bring them through each storm. He is powerful enough to help us withstand each problem in life and bring us through safely.

ABIJAH

Hezekiah was twenty-five years old when he became king,
and he reigned in Jerusalem twenty-nine years.
His mother's name was Abijah daughter of Zechariah.
2 CHRONICLES 29:1

There are not many references to Abijah in scripture, but a very important one commends her son, the king of Judah: "Hezekiah trusted in the LORD, the God of Israel. There was no one like him among all the kings of Judah, either before him or after him" (2 Kings 18:5). Abijah's husband, Ahaz, surely never influenced his son to trust in God, for he increasingly worshiped the pagan gods and even closed Jerusalem's temple. If either of Hezekiah's parents positively influenced his faith, it would have been Abijah.

No matter what a child has experienced, one faithful parent can have a powerful influence for God. While her husband gave himself over to pagan gods, Abijah's quiet faith may have turned her son to the Lord. It is no different today. God still raises up the children of faithful mothers. The unfaithfulness of a father can even become a clear warning and sad contrast to a mother's faith.

No matter what challenges a mother faces, Father God always remains with her, if she trusts in Him and prays faithfully for her child. Though a human father may fail, our Lord never will.

ABISHAG

Then they searched throughout Israel
for a beautiful girl and found Abishag,
a Shunammite, and brought her to the king.
1 KINGS 1:3

Abishag had an unusual job: keeping the old and infirm King David warm. And not just by covering him with blankets—the comely Abishag was expected to crawl into bed with the king. David's servants said to him, "Let her lie in thy bosom, that my lord the king may get heat" (1 Kings 1:2 KJV). That's exactly what happened, as Abishag "ministered" to David in a nonsexual way.

We have no biblical record of Abishag's feelings toward her job. Perhaps she was pleased to be chosen as the great king's personal body warmer. Maybe she found lying in bed with a dying seventy-year old man distasteful. Possibly, her feelings shifted from day to day.

Our feelings toward our own responsibilities—at home, at church, at the office, wherever—can vary widely. But whatever we've been called to do, we should do to the best of our abilities. As the apostle Paul wrote to the church in Corinth, "Now it is required that those who have been given a trust must prove faithful" (1 Corinthians 4:2).

Dream job or nightmare, know that God has called you to this particular time and place. Do your best—and, if appropriate, pray for the chance to move on.

ACSAH

*And Caleb said, "I will give my daughter Acsah in marriage
to the man who attacks and captures Kiriath Sepher."
Othniel son of Kenaz, Caleb's younger brother, took it;
so Caleb gave his daughter Acsah to him in marriage.*

JUDGES 1:12–13

Caleb's declaration seems strange to us. How could he
almost raffle off his daughter to the man who was successful in battle? But in Israel a victory in battle could pay off
the bride price, which was owed to the father before the
marriage. So maybe the man who really wanted her got her
through his bravery.

And the man who won Acsah would have been a good
choice as a husband. Othniel became the first major judge
of Israel, the leader who freed the nation from subjection to
Cushan-Rishathaim, king of Aram (see Judges 3:8–9).

As part of her dowry, Acsah received dry land in the
Negev. So she told her husband to ask Caleb for another
field, one that had springs. When Othniel didn't do it, Acsah
took on the task herself and got the land. Surely Caleb was a
loving father, being generous with his daughter.

What did Acsah think about this marriage? We don't
know. Sometimes brides were asked for their consent, or
perhaps Caleb saw this as a way to give her the man she
wanted without asking money from his brother. Either
way, what a method for finding a good man! No woman
today would think of it.

Like Acsah, we may find romance in unexpected places. Let's remember to let God do the choosing for us—and no matter what the time or situation, we will be blessed. After all, look at the husband Acsah got.

ADAH

Lamech married two women,
one named Adah and the other Zillah.
GENESIS 4:19

Lamech, a man of Cain's line, became the first polygamist in Hebrew history, marrying both Adah and Zillah. Though it might have seemed fun for him, what a wreck it made of women's lives for centuries. For though he was the first to do it, he was hardly the last Hebrew to think more wives were better. From his example came a long history of marital confusion, conflict, and disobedience to God.

The Bible describes Adah and Zillah's children, but does not tell us how their mothers got along. Yet if Hebrew family history is any example, they probably didn't have a smooth life. For God intentionally commanded that one man should marry one woman (see Genesis 2:23–24). Those who disobey God pay a price, so marital harmony probably wasn't a part of this tenthold.

Lamech's rebelliousness didn't limit itself to marriage. He took vengeance by killing a man who wounded him. Like Cain, he overreacted and failed to seek God's counsels.

From Adah's story we learn the importance of following God's laws. What must it have been like to live with this angry man? And how could Adah share her husband with Zillah, yet understand God's complete commitment to those who love Him?

This quick picture of Adah's life teaches us to let God control our marital choices. In Him, we'll experience the warm, loving relationship we're looking for. Apart from Him, we may feel only pain.

AHINOAM

Abigail. . .went with David's messengers and became his wife.
David had also married Ahinoam of Jezreel,
and they both were his wives.
1 SAMUEL 25:42–43

Nearly every time the Bible mentions Ahinoam, David's other wife, Abigail, appears, too. Though Ahinoam was first married to David, the wealthy Abigail seems to overshadow her. Ahinoam didn't even come from an impressive city, for Jezreel was only a town in the hill country of Judah. Since her name means "gracious," perhaps Ahinoam never made trouble—but she had to feel slighted.

With David and Abigail, she traveled to find protection among the Philistines, so Saul could not destroy her husband. While David went to war at the Philistine king Achish's side, the Amalekites raided his home at Ziklag, capturing Ahinoam and Abigail. David returned early to rescue the women. What a joyous moment it must have been for Ahinoam to see her husband and his troops, for she might otherwise have become a slave.

After Saul died, David became king of Judah, and Ahinoam bore his son Amnon. Amnon would grow up to dishonor his half-sister Tamar, but Ahinoam may never have known that—since she's not mentioned in the story, she may no longer have been living.

Ahinoam has only a small part in biblical history, though she was the wife of a king. She may have been quiet and faithful, getting less press than David's other wives. Like Ahinoam, can we take a backseat? Or would we become resentful, needing front-page attention to be satisfied?

ANNA

There was also a prophetess, Anna,
the daughter of Phanuel, of the tribe of Asher.
She was very old; she had lived with her husband
seven years after her marriage,
and then was a widow until she was eighty-four.
She never left the temple but worshiped night and day,
fasting and praying.
Coming up to them at that very moment,
she gave thanks to God
and spoke about the child to all who were
looking forward to the redemption of Jerusalem.

LUKE 2:36–38

This is all we know of Anna—you've just read the whole biblical account of her. But it is enough to give a thumbnail sketch of her character and devotion to God.

Her name means "gracious," and grace seems to have permeated her life. She married, but after her husband died, she dedicated the rest of her life to God. Hers was a service of many years; at eighty-four, this widow was still constantly in the temple. She may have lived within the temple confines or perhaps lived nearby and simply spent most of her time "at church." Certainly her fellow Jews would have honored her for remaining single and dedicating her life in devotion to her Lord.

As a prophetess, Anna held a position of honor. Clearly, God spoke to her as she remained in the temple, worshiping, fasting, and praying. Is it any wonder that when the Messiah first entered the temple, she walked in on Him and His parents? Surely God led her there, to be blessed by the sight of the One she had long hoped for. Immediately recognizing Jesus, she thanked her heavenly Father and spread the news to others.

Like Anna, do we need to remain single and live in the church? Hardly. But whether we are married or single, we need to ask if we share her single-hearted devotion to God. Are our spirits so tuned to His voice that we hear and obey His call in our lives? When His Spirit whispers to us, is that still, small voice drowned out by the cares of the world, or are we so attuned to Him that we can obey at a moment's notice?

When we share Anna's ability to obey, we'll discover how gracious God has been to us. His spiritual blessings will spill over into our lives and others', too.

ATHALIAH

When Athaliah the mother of Ahaziah
saw that her son was dead,
she proceeded to destroy the whole royal family
of the house of Judah.

2 CHRONICLES 22:10

Athaliah, daughter of Israel's wicked king Ahab, is one of
the bad babes of the Bible. Instead of being a godly mother,
scripture tells us she encouraged her son, Ahaziah, to do
wrong (see 2 Chronicles 22:3). After becoming king of
Judah, Ahaziah joined his uncle Joram, king of Israel, in a
battle against Hazael, king of Aram. Following the battle,
the warrior Jehu, who had already killed many of Ahaziah's
heirs, wiped out Judah's king, too.

When Athaliah heard the news, she immediately sought
to kill off all her grandchildren so she could gain the
throne. Once she did that, her claim would be reasonably
uncontested. This power-hungry woman literally sacrificed
her family on the altar of her own ambition.

Had she been successful, the line of the Messiah
would have been destroyed. So God placed a faithful
woman, Jehosheba, near Ahaziah's son Joash. This half
sister of the dead king saved her nephew and his nurse,
hiding them in a bedroom. For six years the child king
remained in hiding at the temple while his grandmother
ruled (see 2 Kings 11:2–4).

In the seventh year of Athaliah's rule, the priest

Jehoiada introduced Joash to the Israelite war commanders. They covenanted with Joash and protected him while Jehoiada anointed him king. Hearing heard the noise of her grandson's coronation, Athaliah called out, "Treason!" but the troops ignored her objections and obeyed the priest. Removing her from the temple, they took her life in Jerusalem's Horse Gate.

Athaliah's actions are shocking. Few of us would sacrifice our children or grandchildren to gain power. But sometimes our fast-paced, twenty-first century existence causes us to shortchange our family of time and attention. If our jobs always come first, we travel incessantly, or we place our children too often in the hands of others, perhaps we've begun to make the same mistake as this wicked queen. We don't have to serve a pagan god or want to rule a nation in order to get our priorities mixed up.

If we fail, we aren't bad babes in the mold of an Athaliah—but we do need to repent, confess our wrongdoing, and find a way to make changes. Maybe that means reorganizing our time, refusing a promotion, or working a part-time job. Whatever it takes, let's not sacrifice our families to get ahead. Because, in the end, we won't be ahead at all—either with our loved ones or the God we serve.

BATHSHEBA

One evening David got up from his bed
and walked around on the roof of the palace.
From the roof he saw a woman bathing.
The woman was very beautiful,
and David sent someone to find out about her.
The man said, "Isn't this Bathsheba,
the daughter of Eliam
and the wife of Uriah the Hittite?"

2 SAMUEL 11:2–3

Bathsheba must have been a real looker—a king was unable to resist her when he got a look at her from the roof of his palace. David sent messengers to bring the Hittite's wife to him, and then David slept with her.

Scripture never seems to ask how Bathsheba felt about this. Was she offended at being commandeered by a king, or was she flattered that he had noticed her? Whatever her response, she didn't have any say in her situation.

Then, to her horror, Bathsheba discovered she was pregnant. In Jewish law, the punishment for adultery was death for both the man and woman. Fear must have struck this beauty's heart. Even if she thought to pass the child off as her husband's, Uriah had been away at war and surely would know the child was not his. So she told David, and the king came up with a solution. He called Uriah back to Jerusalem, assuming Bathsheba could entice him into a romantic interlude—and the problem would be solved.

But the king, who had fallen into this sin when he should have been on the battlefield, did not count on the uprightness of this foreigner who had taken the Jewish faith to heart. Coming to the king as ordered, Uriah refused to so much as cross his own threshold. When others were camping out, readying for war, he would not sleep with his wife in Jerusalem. David made him drunk, but he still would not go home. Seeing no other alternative, and perhaps feeling growing guilt over his own sins, the king changed plans, commanding that Uriah should be placed in the heat of battle and left defenseless. The plan worked: Uriah died.

Bathsheba lost her husband at the connivance of her lover. Perhaps she initially felt relief at getting out of a very tight situation. But if her husband treated her tenderly, as Nathan's accusation of David in 2 Samuel 12:3 implies, she must at least have felt some emotional conflict.

When Bathsheba's short period of mourning ended, David made her his wife. In a few months, she gave him a son. Though the Bible never blames Bathsheba for the sin between herself and the king, she shared in his grief when God punished David by taking the life of their child. But God quickly blessed her with another son, Solomon, who was loved by God and would become one of Israel's greatest kings. She also had three more children (see 1 Chronicles 3:5).

Years later, Bathsheba stood up for her son's right to become king of Israel, when his older brother Adonijah sought to grab the throne from the aging David (see

1 Kings 1:5–21). At her request, David kept his promise to make Solomon king (see verse 29).

Still, Bathsheba must have been more kindhearted than politically savvy, for when Adonijah asked to marry Abishag, who'd been David's nurse in his old age, Bathsheba pled his case to Solomon. Solomon deeply loved his mother, if the great respect he treated her with is any sign (see 1 Kings 2:19). But he immediately saw that his brother was again threatening his throne, denied her mission, and had his brother killed.

Bathsheba's story is that of the second chance. Her life was turned upside down by a king's desire, and she was seduced into sin with him. But she didn't stay there. God gave her another chance as David's wife, and the rest of the biblical account shows her as a caring mother and concerned wife. No one accused her of further sin, and she lived blamelessly.

When God gives us second chances, we can follow in Bathsheba's footsteps. As long as we are alive, we are on a mission for Him. Will we make ours as successful as hers? Remember this: Bathsheba is one of only four women mentioned in the lineage of Jesus (see Matthew 1:6).

BILHAH

*Laban gave his servant girl Bilhah
to his daughter Rachel as her maidservant.*
GENESIS 29:29

Had Bilhah known what this change in her life would mean, perhaps she would have run the other way. For serving Rachel meant more than looking after her and running her errands. When Rachel did not have children, she decided her husband, Jacob, should follow a custom of the day and take Bilhah as a concubine. According to the custom, Rachel would adopt Bilhah's children as her own. But instead of establishing a happy family, Rachel began a competition with her sister, Leah, Jacob's other wife, who had borne him four children. Eventually their face-off saddled Jacob with twelve sons and a far-from-peaceful household, disrupted by two wives and two concubines, Bilhah and Zilpah. Though God used Bilhah to raise up some of Jacob's sons, who would eventually become leaders of the twelve tribes of Israel, her role was not a thoroughly pleasant one.

God established marriage as between one man and one woman (see Genesis 2:24) to reflect His covenant. Ignore that, and your family life, like Jacob's, can become as confused as the plot of a modern-day soap opera. But God blesses marriages that reflect His covenant love. Faithful love ends soap-opera lives and establishes a firm family that can serve God well. Would that describe your family? If not, what can you change?

CANDACE

So he started out, and on his way
he met an Ethiopian eunuch, an important official
in charge of all the treasury of Candace,
queen of the Ethiopians.
This man had gone to Jerusalem to worship.

ACTS 8:27

In the first century, unlike today, *Candace* was not a name, but a title. It belonged to the queen mother of the ruler of an area the Greeks called Meroe, around the upper reaches of the Nile River. The people of that nation felt the king was so holy he was good for nothing temporal, so Candace carried out many of his earthly responsibilities. As a trade center, her country was very wealthy, so her powerful official in charge of the treasury would have had the ability to travel to the Holy City for worship.

From this trip, he brought back more than Candace would have expected—the news of the Messiah struck the Ethiopian eunuch's heart quickly, and he accepted Christ. According to tradition, the woman he served also accepted Christ.

We never know, when we share our faith, what important person may be touched by our words. Though our friends might be humble, we may connect with a powerful man or woman who needs to come to faith. With a single witness, like Phillip, God's Word may reach a person of influence. Speak up!

CHLOE

*My brothers, some from Chloe's household
have informed me that there are quarrels among you.*
1 CORINTHIANS 1:11

We don't really know anything more about Chloe or her household than this verse reveals, but she was probably an important woman, since she's named as the head of her household. And we know a lot about her church from Paul's letters to the Corinthians.

Chloe didn't belong to a perfect congregation—division, not unity, was the hallmark of the Corinthian church. Everyone wanted to choose a leader to follow: Paul, Apollos, Peter (Cephas), or Christ. No one seemed to be in charge.

Obviously some faithful believer from Chloe's household, perhaps even Chloe herself, became troubled by the quarrels that divided the Corinthian church. A report got back to Paul that these foolish arguments had separated believers. When he heard, he confronted the young Corinthian Christians, even generally naming the source of his information. Because Paul received this report, he was able to save the church from an implosion.

Should we find ourselves in her situation, Chloe gives us an example. *Do we drop a word in a church leader's ear or keep it to ourselves?* we wonder. God provides us with the wisdom for each problem we face. By speaking now, we could defuse a serious problem later.

COZBI

And the name of the Midianite woman
who was put to death was Cozbi daughter of Zur,
a tribal chief of a Midianite family.
NUMBERS 25:15

Her name means "deceitful," and deceit had helped her seduce the Israelite leader Zimri. But it doesn't seem Zimri was slow in following her, and he wasn't the only one of his people who fell. Many followed the Moabite and Midianite women into sexual sin while worshiping their idols.

God's anger burned brightly against His people, and retribution followed. He commanded Moses to kill the leaders and show off their bodies to His people. Meanwhile a plague broke out among the Israelites, perhaps to give them a picture of the deadliness of their sin.

At that moment, in front of everyone, Zimri led Cozbi, the daughter of a Midianite chief, into a tent—the sort of place for prostitutes. While the rest of Israel repented of their sins, Zimri marched right by the whole assembly of Israel, ready to continue his wrongdoing.

Aaron's grandson, Phinehas, quickly took care of the problem by running a spear through the couple's bodies, taking their lives. With the deaths of this willfully disobedient pair, the plague on Israel stopped—but not before twenty-four thousand people died.

Cozbi shows us that sin doesn't pay. God may be patient with us, but He does not wink at disobedience. If we boldly continue in sin, it will eventually bring terrible judgment. Worse yet, our wrongs may affect many innocent lives as well as our own. Are we willing to take that risk?

DAMARIS

A few men became followers of Paul and believed. Among them was Dionysius, a member of the Areopagus, also a woman named Damaris, and a number of others.
ACTS 17:34

Luke mentions some men who accepted Christ as their Savior when they heard Paul's message in Athens, then suddenly he drops in the name of a woman: Damaris. Perhaps, as John Chrysostom, a fourth-century archbishop of Constantinople, thought, she was the wife of Dionysius. Others suggest she was an important, educated woman, perhaps from another country. But in an age when women rarely got much mention, she must have had some stature to be listed immediately after a member of Athens' ruling council. Indeed, for her to be present at the meeting where Paul spoke would indicate she had some unusual importance.

The next time someone tells you women aren't important in the Bible, remind them of Damaris, Priscilla, and the Marys of the Gospels. People may write women off as being unimportant, but God never does. He includes them at every point in His story of redemption.

You, too, are important to God. Whether or not you're ever mentioned in a book or known worldwide, God cares for you. His Son died for you, to draw you to His side. No one for whom Jesus died is unimportant or forgotten.

THE DAUGHTER OF PHARAOH

Then Pharaoh's daughter went down to the Nile to bathe,
and her attendants were walking along the river bank.
She saw the basket among the reeds
and sent her slave girl to get it.
She opened it and saw the baby.
He was crying, and she felt sorry for him.
"This is one of the Hebrew babies," she said.
EXODUS 2:5–6

Being important doesn't mean everyone knows you. Though this woman was the daughter of Egypt's powerful ruler, the Bible never records her name or even that of her father. All we know of Pharaoh's daughter is her position and the fact that she had a kind spirit, for when she saw the baby Moses floating in a basket, her heart opened to him. The woman knew he was one of the Hebrews whom Pharaoh had commanded to be killed, yet this woman disobeyed her father and bravely saved the baby, who ironically became the prophet God used to free the Hebrews from Egypt's grasp.

In time, the princess adopted Moses, opening doors

of education and power to the young Hebrew. Because of the training he received in Egypt's court, he was probably in a better position to rule over the rebellious Hebrews. As an educated man, he would be able to record the first five books of the Bible for all people to read through the ages.

Though we don't know that she ever came to faith, the princess played an important role in God's plan. Without her, the tiny baby would not have had the advantages he needed. But God placed the right woman in the right place at the right time, and He moved her heart to help young Moses. Her name may have disappeared, but her good work hasn't.

We're probably all familiar with someone who doesn't know God but performs many good deeds. An unsaved family member may help us out and enable us to fulfill God's will in our lives. Do we recognize that this, too, comes from God? God may use many different people to accomplish His goal, but He does not abuse them. He never forces them to have faith in Him.

Many daughters of Pharaoh live in our midst, unconsciously guided by their Creator to do His will. Yet they have no spiritual connection to Him. Do we reach out to them, hoping to help them understand His role in their lives? We can rejoice when they come to know Him, too.

DEBORAH, REBEKAH'S NURSE

Now Deborah, Rebekah's nurse,
died and was buried under the oak below Bethel.
So it was named Allon Bacuth.

GENESIS 35:8

Did you know the name of Rebekah's nurse? Genesis 24:59 told us she accompanied her charge to their new home with Jacob, but it did not mention the nurse's name. Now, at Deborah's death, we finally can put a name with a position.

Deborah spent plenty of years with her mistress. Perhaps Rebekah appreciated Deborah's kindness to her when she was tiny. Rebekah would have still needed her nurse as she grew, because Genesis 29:29 makes it obvious the bride had no maid. For awhile after Rebekah's marriage there were no children to change in the middle of the night, but Deborah helped her charge settle into a new way of life. When children did come, Rebekah desperately needed the nurse, since she had twins. Deborah was always there to dandle a crying child or wrap him in a blanket.

Many of us have received help with our children from a friend, teacher, or youth-group worker. Do we appreciate the effort that goes into caring for children? Like Deborah, many give tender care to youngsters who are not theirs. Will it be a thankless task or one that receives appreciation? Rebekah appreciated her nurse: The name of that oak under which Deborah was buried became Allon Bacuth: "oak of weeping."

DEBORAH THE PROPHETESS

Deborah, a prophetess, the wife of Lappidoth,
was leading Israel at that time.
She held court under the Palm of Deborah
between Ramah and Bethel
in the hill country of Ephraim,
and the Israelites came to her
to have their disputes decided.

JUDGES 4:4–5

God doesn't explain Himself. Suddenly, in a time when Israel has become unfaithful to the Lord, the scripture proclaims the position of Deborah, the only female to rule Israel during the years of the judges—that era between Joshua's death and Saul's accession as king. Deborah was not just a minor judge; she was an authoritative woman who decided disputes between men and held the power common to all Israel's judges. Nor was this a piece-of-cake leadership for Deborah. Israel had been subjugated by the Canaanite ruler Jabin of Hazor, yet the Israelites never brought an army against him until this woman was in charge. Deborah became the answer to the prayer for help her people sent up to God as they saw the Canaanite commander Sisera heading their direction followed by nine hundred chariots.

God had chosen an unusual leader in Deborah, a very strong-minded woman who was also very close to Him. (Just read her interaction with her military commander,

Barak, in Judges 4:6–9, and you'll see she was used to being obeyed.) As a prophetess, Deborah would have heard and communicated God's will to His people. Though she is not the only prophetess in the Bible, she alone ruled Israel. Not only that, she effectively led her country during wartime, when many people might have chosen a man for the job. After all, she couldn't command an army, could she? In a way, she showed the doubters that she could.

God had given her authority, and Deborah obeyed His will implicitly. Maybe you've known a powerful woman like her. An in-charge kind of person, this judge rallied her leaders and the people against the Canaanites. Barak, chosen by God as the country's military commander, seems shy and retiring compared to the confident prophetess. God spoke to her, and she told Barak all He had commanded. Deborah did not make decisions based on her own desires, but on God's direction for His people. And she showed greater faith than her commander. She was probably a "God says it, I've heard it, that settles it" kind of believer, because she did not understand why Barak balked at going to war when God told him to. Barak flatly refused to go to battle without Deborah. That may have been fueled in part by an understanding that following her was following God, but doubt also played its role. Because of Barak's hesitancy, God commanded that a woman would take the life of Sisera.

Deborah accompanied the ten thousand troops who attacked Sisera's forces and gave them the order to go into battle on God's chosen day. When Barak and his men obeyed, God caused the Canaanites to flee before them. But this was something other than Barak's happiest moment. Deborah's prophecy of Sisera's death was fulfilled when Jael, a woman, killed Sisera in her tent, after all the Canaanite troops had been destroyed.

Judges 5 records Deborah's wonderful song celebrating the victory. Together with Barak, she gave the credit to God. From her verses we get a clear picture of how sad life had been like under the Canaanites. She described herself as "a mother in Israel," but she had also been something of a mother *to* Israel, encouraging, warning, and setting the pace for a whole nation. She praised Jael for killing the enemy with tent peg and hammer. Through Jael, God ended the fighting and gave Israel a complete victory.

Need a picture of a confident, powerful woman who was also humble and faithful? Look to Deborah. Being an unlikely leader didn't stop her in her tracks, and it doesn't need to stop a Christian woman today, either. She can be a successful mother, leader, and wife, if she's obeying God every day.

DELILAH

*Some time later, he fell in love with a woman
in the Valley of Sorek whose name was Delilah.*
JUDGES 16:4

Say her name, and most Christians get an immediate picture of a sultry woman and desire gone wrong.

The physically powerful Israelite judge Samson fell for this beautiful and desirable Philistine. As wise as he must have been, Samson had one fatal flaw: He never chose well when it came to women—those foreign temptresses forbidden by God's Law always seemed to claim his attention. His marriage to a Philistine woman had ended disastrously, yet here he was, becoming romantic with Delilah. Maybe he thought it was okay as long as they didn't marry, but He should have read his Law a bit more carefully.

No sooner had Samson fallen for this bad babe than the rulers of her nation asked Delilah to do some spying for them. The Israelite was so strong that they couldn't capture him, and they had a series of grudges against him. So they asked Delilah to find out what made her lover so powerful. Once they had his secret, the rulers planned to make him a slave.

Maybe it was the money that made this bad girl decide Samson was expendable. Eleven hundred shekels from each of five rulers was no small amount of cash in that day. Delilah must have decided that all she needed was money, not love, and in her greed, she betrayed Samson completely.

At the same time, you have to wonder what Samson was thinking. Perhaps he enjoyed playing romantic games, but didn't he get the least bit suspicious when his beloved asked how his strength could be subdued? Didn't he figure that she was a Philistine and that others could be putting her up to something? He'd had a very similar experience with his wife, before their marriage fell apart, so you'd think he had to have had an inkling, especially when he gave Delilah three false answers. You wonder how many times God had to show Samson the same lesson for him to learn.

But when Samson should have left off dallying with Delilah, he kept coming around—giving her the opportunity to nag him endlessly. "You don't love me," she complained, and evidently he couldn't bear to see her unhappy. Eventually she wore him down, and he admitted that his vow as a Nazirite—and the long hair that was part of it—gave him his strength. Cut his hair, he said, and he'd be weak as any other man.

The Philistines took complete advantage of this information. Delilah got Samson to sleep in her lap, and a man came in to shave his head. Awakened, Samson soon stood powerless, and the Philistines made him a sightless slave. But these temporary victors forgot that hair grows again! And grow it did.

Inside their temple, the Philistine rulers and an assembly gathered to rejoice at the capture of Israel's strong man. In the midst of their reveling, the crowd called Samson out to perform for them.

"Now the temple was crowded with men and women; all the rulers of the Philistines were there, and on the roof were about three thousand men and women watching Samson perform" (Judges 16:27). Adorned with a new head of hair and imbued with renewed strength, Samson stood before them, prayed for strength, pushed against the pillars with all his might, and brought down the pagan temple, killing himself and everyone in it.

Who knows if Delilah was also there amid the crowd? Though she didn't seem like the religious kind, perhaps she had taken that opportunity to rejoice at the effectiveness of her sexual powers.

Look at Delilah, and you get a clear picture of how *not* to live. Need an example of what loose living will get you? She's the poster child for it. The pain she caused someone who loved her ran so deep that Samson didn't mind sacrificing his life, if he could destroy the pagan temple he'd been taken to. Samson had been used by an immoral woman who evidently felt no guilt at betraying him.

Delilah backs up God's Word, which commands a faithful husband-and-wife lifestyle. Romance is not a game, but a lifelong commitment. And any sexual activity outside marriage leads to heartbreak. Maybe yours won't come as quickly as Samson's did, and you may not die, but you can count on some pain when you don't live God's way.

Just ask Delilah—if you can find her under all that rubble, that is.

DIANA

So that not only this our craft is in danger to be set at nought;
but also that the temple of the great goddess
Diana should be despised,
and her magnificence should be destroyed,
whom all Asia and the world worshippeth.

ACTS 19:27 KJV

Diana, also known as Artemis of the Ephesians, isn't, strictly speaking, a woman. She was a pagan fertility goddess who got the apostle Paul and his disciples into a lot of trouble. When Paul's ministry to Asia took off, Ephesian craftsman Demetrius the silversmith saw his nice little business of creating Diana idols going down the drain. So he called a guild meeting and got the backing of his fellow silversmiths to take action.

If they didn't act, the magnificent temple of Diana would suffer, the silversmith warned. Today that temple is known as one of the seven wonders of the ancient world. In Demetrius's day, thousands of pilgrims flooded Ephesus to worship there, but he knew they wouldn't if the pilgrims became Christians. So Demetrius and his coworkers started a riot. Only the intervention of the city clerk saved Paul and his men, and Paul wisely moved on to Macedonia.

Diana led a lot of people into idolatry and away from the gospel. But her magnificence and her following only lasted a short time. After all, no one worships her today. Are you putting your faith in something that won't last long or the God who created the universe and will never fail you? Don't follow a Diana, when you can draw close to the eternal Lord.

DINAH

*Now Dinah, the daughter Leah had borne to Jacob,
went out to visit the women of the land.*
GENESIS 34:1

In this simple sentence begins one of the saddest events of the book of Genesis. Dinah, a young and thoughtless girl, comes to a new country and unwisely goes out to seek friendship with the pagan women there. On the way, she is raped by Shechem, son of Hamor the Canaanite who was ruler of the city that shares his son's name. Afterward, when young Shechem belatedly decides to marry Dinah, he unknowingly brings disaster on his people.

Hamor, pushed on by his son, approaches Jacob to arrange a marriage. It was a common practice of that day, and the heartbroken Jacob listens. But before he makes a decision, Jacob's furious sons intervene. How can they give their sister to an unbelieving man? Surely Jacob must have struggled with this idea, since his father had commanded him not to marry a Canaanite—but what could he do that would benefit his daughter? Though Jacob is unaware of it, his sons come up with a wicked suggestion: If the Canaanites will accept circumcision, Jacob's sons inform

Hamor and Shechem, they will accept the marriage. But there's more to their offer than meets the eye.

Hamor agrees, but not because he's had a sudden conversion experience—he's interested in getting his hands on Jacob's wealth, the large herd of sheep in his possession. But the ruler has not reckoned with the brothers' anger. The siblings plot to kill the male Shechemites while they are still in pain from the surgery. Three days after the circumcision rite, Simeon and Levi, Dinah's full brothers, begin the attack on the city. All the male Shechemites are killed, and the Israelites loot the city. In order to keep his family safe, an angry Jacob moves his family out of the area.

Double sorrow was Dinah's: her rape and her brothers' precipitate actions. Scripture gives us no clue about her life after this event, but it was surely changed forever. Dinah's life shows us that sometimes even simple, foolish decisions impact us powerfully. We need to be careful how we walk and with whom we associate.

DORCAS

In Joppa there was a disciple named Tabitha
(which, when translated, is Dorcas),
who was always doing good and helping the poor.
ACTS 9:36

This faithful woman lived in the seaport city of Joppa,
outside today's city of Tel Aviv. *Dorcas* was actually a
Greek translation of her Aramean name, *Tabitha*, which
means "gazelle." Scripture doesn't tell us if her frame
matched her name, but it does say she leapt to do good
works for others.

While Peter was visiting nearby, Dorcas died. Her fellow Christians readied her for burial and sent a message to
the apostle, who hurried to them. The sorrowing believers
showed him examples of Dorcas's generosity. After clearing
the room, the apostle raised Dorcas from the dead. What a
day that must have been for Dorcas, the other Christians,
and even for those who heard about the miracle and came
to faith in Christ.

Do our lives testify to our faith as clearly as Dorcas's
did? Living, dying, or being resurrected, she glorified her
Lord. If we died, would our fellow Christians want to have
us back as a powerful Christian testimony?

DRUSILLA

*Several days later Felix came with his wife Drusilla,
who was a Jewess. He sent for Paul and listened to him
as he spoke about faith in Christ Jesus.*

Acts 24:24

Drusilla may have been a Jewess, but she wasn't a very
faithful one. Felix was not her first husband—after only a
year of marriage, she had left her husband Azizus, king of
Emesa, to go with Felix.

Perhaps this lack of faith isn't surprising, consider-
ing her background. Drusilla was a great-granddaughter
of Herod the Great and daughter of Herod Agrippa I.
Ruthlessness, not belief, was a hallmark of her family.

When the Jewish leaders brought Paul to Felix,
demanding that he be punished for troublemaking, Paul
took the opportunity to witness to Felix and his wife. They
never came to faith, perhaps because they had another
agenda—Felix was hoping for a bribe, not seeking the
truth. Perhaps his wife had the same attitude.

It does not matter if we come from a long line of faithless people. Each of us has an opportunity to accept Christ
through a personal witness, a book, or the testimony of a
preacher. Will we remain in a godless past or reach out to
Jesus through faith? It's our choice alone.

ELISHEBA

Aaron married Elisheba,
daughter of Amminadab and sister of Nahshon,
and she bore him Nadab and Abihu,
Eleazar and Ithamar.

EXODUS 6:23

Aaron's wife doesn't get a lot of press in the Bible. Her brother Nahshon gets more mention as a leader of the tribe of Judah, but Elisheba would have been well known to the Israelites, as wife of their high priest.

Elisheba had a wonderful husband, but her children were another matter. Leviticus 10:1–2 describes the death of her first two sons, Nadab and Abihu. Instead of following God's directions in worship, they pridefully made an unauthorized incense offering. As punishment, God consumed them with fire. Some scholars suspect that Nadab and Abihu had been drunk at the time, a condition which led them to take such unholy actions. The scholars' reasoning comes from the fact that soon after this incident, God warned Aaron and his sons not to drink before worship (see Leviticus 10:9).

Not every woman of God has children who make her proud. Every child is different, and while one may delight a mother, another may bring much sorrow. Christian mothers may faithfully witness to their children, yet be unable to turn them away from wrongdoing.

But, as in the case of Elisheba, God may also provide a

believing mother with a great blessing. Eleazar, Elisheba's third son, honored his parents' faith, following in his father's footsteps. He became the head of the Levites and then high priest in Aaron's place.

ELIZABETH

But they had no children,
because Elizabeth was barren;
and they were both well along in years.

LUKE 1:7

The godly Zechariah and his wife, Elizabeth, both from the priestly line, were aging people who seemed unable to have children. What a shock, then, for Zechariah to receive a visit from an angel who told him he and Elizabeth would have a son, John.

Is it any wonder Zechariah doubted? But saying the equivalent of "Oh, no, you must be wrong" to an angel? What was he thinking? God showed a sense of humor, making the expectant father unable to speak until the birth of the promised child—perhaps so he wouldn't say any other silly things.

Some time later, Mary visited Elizabeth. Mary's relative immediately knew this young woman would bear the Messiah and praised her Lord for it. What a time of fellowship this must have been for these women who bore children with missions unlike any others in the world.

When Elizabeth had her son, the relatives assumed the couple would follow custom by naming him after his father, Zechariah. But the angel had declared his name would be John, and that's what Elizabeth called the boy. The family questioned the father. As soon as he wrote, "His name is John," Zechariah's mouth was opened and he praised the Lord. From that moment on, all could see that John was somehow special. They wondered what the Lord would do with his life.

Elizabeth must have been amazed at the turn life took for her. Long accustomed to being thought barren, she was suddenly given a special child who would serve God in an unusual way. How blessed she must have felt!

When life takes unexpected turns for us, will we be a doubting Zechariah or a faithful Elizabeth? Trusting God takes a lot of faith when our lives are suddenly turned upside down. We have two choices: We can simply allow God to control whatever happens, or we can spend time worrying about the future.

Since we can't change the future—and God has it all under control anyway—we may as well follow Elizabeth's example. We, too, may find God has given us unexpected blessings.

ESTHER

Mordecai had a cousin named Hadassah,
whom he had brought up because
she had neither father nor mother.
This girl, who was also known as Esther,
was lovely in form and features,
and Mordecai had taken her as his own daughter
when her father and mother died.

ESTHER 2:7

Displeased with his queen, Vashti, King Xerxes of Persia
put her aside to seek out another. After a nationwide
search, his eye lit on a woman who had been exiled to his
land. But Esther never told the king about her Jewish family
background.

Perhaps Xerxes's find-a-queen contest was fun. With
many other girls, Esther was brought to the court and
given beauty treatments. Maids waited on her. Then came
the night when Esther was sent to the king as his concubine. Though He is never mentioned in this book of the
Bible, God certainly guided Esther's life—for of all the
women, she was most attractive to this far-from-virtuous
king. Xerxes made her queen.

In time, Esther's cousin, Mordecai, uncovered an assassination plot against the king. But instead of honoring the
Jew, the king raised his courtier Haman to the highest position among the nobles. When Mordecai refused to bow
down to Haman, the king's favorite hatched a plot to rid

himself of Mordecai and the Jewish people. Haman got the king's unwitting approval to wipe out his queen's race.

Mordecai revealed Haman's plan to Esther and told her to go to the king. Since anyone who approached the king without invitation could be put to death—and Esther had not been called for a month—the queen feared for her life.

Mordecai warned her, "Do not think that because you are in the king's house you alone of all the Jews will escape. For if you remain silent at this time, relief and deliverance for the Jews will arise from another place, but you and your father's family will perish. And who knows but that you have come to royal position for such a time as this?" (Esther 4:13–14). Esther promised to go, if her cousin would fast and pray for her.

Esther went before the king, who spared her life and offered to do anything she wanted. She asked only that he and Haman attend two banquets—one that day and the other on the morrow. Though thrilled to be so honored, Haman's attitude soured when he saw Mordecai again. A furious Haman ordered a gallows built for his enemy.

That night, an insomniac Xerxes had the record of his reign read to him—and discovered that Mordecai had never been rewarded for his faithfulness. In an amusing turn of God's plan, the king asked Haman what should be done to someone the king wished to honor. Haman, assuming that person was himself, suggested a kingly robe and a royal horse be brought, and that a nobleman lead the honored man through the city, declaring why the king was honoring him. What a shock to Haman when he was the nobleman commanded to honor Mordecai that way! But Haman had to obey.

When Haman attended the queen's second banquet, Esther revealed the plot to the shocked Xerxes. The king commanded his courtier be immediately hanged on the gallows built for Mordecai—and ordered Mordecai to write a new law protecting the Jews. So for one day, the Jews were able to fight off their enemies. They killed every one, leaving their people safe and instituting the holiday of Purim.

God's name is absent from Esther's book, but His hand on her life is apparent. And so it will be with us: When we face trials, we can also trust He is working out something positive on our behalf.

Though becoming a king's concubine may not have seemed good, God watched over Esther so that she became queen. Even our most traumatic moments are also in God's hands. When we trust Him, nothing can go terribly wrong.

Obedient Esther acted on God's will, gave in to her cousin's wise counsel, and was safe. Likewise, God protects us, especially when our faithfulness puts us in danger. If He can stay the hand of a powerful ruler, what will He not do for us?

EUNICE

I have been reminded of your sincere faith,
which first lived in your grandmother Lois
and in your mother Eunice and,
I am persuaded, now lives in you also.
2 TIMOTHY 1:5

For Timothy, faith was a family affair.

His mother was a believing Jewess (see Acts 16:1), and his grandmother also believed. According to the references Paul makes to this young man's family, Timothy had received an important spiritual inheritance, though his father, a Greek, had evidently never come to faith. These two female relatives show how important a woman's witness can be to her children and grandchildren. Despite certain influences of unbelief, a son or grandson can learn from a faithful life lived out before him.

Today, many single moms wonder how they can influence their sons for Christ. They need not fear. God can work in a family where even one member is yielded to him. Obedience, prayer, and the blessings God provides to his faithful people are a powerful influence on a young life. When doubts seemed to trouble Timothy, Paul did not hesitate to remind his young friend of his family history. Clearly, the apostle knew what a powerful influence a mom can be.

EUODIA

I plead with Euodia and I plead with Syntyche
to agree with each other in the Lord. Yes,
and I ask you, loyal yokefellow, help these women
who have contended at my side in the cause of the gospel. . . .
PHILIPPIANS 4:2–3

These verses show us that though these two women had
"contended at [his] side in the cause of the gospel," Paul
felt their contention with each other endangered their
church. Certainly their interpersonal problem was serious enough to deserve a mention in his letter to the
Philippians.

But don't be mistaken: These weren't heretics or women
of small faith. Even sincere, hardworking Christians can
allow contention to separate them. Paul pled with their fellow congregants to help Euodia and Syntyche find a solution to their difference of opinion.

Not much has changed in the years since Paul's ministry
ended. Christians still have heated debates, whether they're
over what color to paint the church or how to witness for
Christ. Paul warned another church, "Do not let the sun go
down while you are still angry" (Ephesians 4:26).

Anger will come, but it need not remain and damage
one's faith, the church, and the Christian witness in the
world. All of us need to quickly talk to each other and end
the anger. If we need help, it's as close as wise counselors in
our congregation.

EVE

Adam named his wife Eve,
because she would become
the mother of all the living.
GENESIS 3:20

The first woman had it made. Specially created by God for her husband, she never had to worry about arguments over who was going to do the dishes or how to spend the family money—there were no such things in Eden. She lived and worked in a beautiful God-planted garden and got to speak to God personally every day. Nothing was wrong with Eve's life.

But one day, a serpent whispered in Eve's ear, tempting her to eat fruit from the one off-limits tree in their beautiful backyard. That crafty snake told Eve that God was holding out on her—if she ate that luscious produce, she'd know good and evil. Though she had no clue what that meant, it sounded interesting to Eve.

Had she been able to see where this was heading, Eve would have stopped that critter in his tracks. But knowing evil looked so good from her perfect place. So not only did she eat the forbidden fruit, she passed it on to Adam, too. The results of her choice, though, weren't quite what she expected. It wasn't as if she suddenly had God's power to know all things—instead, evil entered all human lives through her one bad choice.

Now, when God came into their garden, the couple

disappeared. He had to seek out the embarrassed pair who suddenly understood the impact of a bad choice. How guilty they must have felt! But how could they hide from the Lord of the universe? He cornered them, and the blame game began: Adam blamed Eve; Eve blamed the snake.

All offenders, from the snake on up to Adam, received a curse intimately related to their situation. For Eve, it was pain in childbirth and being ruled by her husband—you might say the "battle of the sexes" started here. For Adam, the curse meant having to work hard to make the land yield a crop. For both, eternal life was now a thing of the past. After God banished Adam and Eve from their lovely garden, He placed a flaming sword to guard their access to the tree of life.

Once outside of Eden, Eve had two sons, first Cain and then Abel. Following the pain of childbirth, she rejoiced at the gifts God had given her—two sons—but sin was already affecting her entire family. The pain of childbirth was just the beginning of her anguish.

As adults, both her sons came to God with an offering. Abel brought the best of his flock, while Cain brought his produce. God approved of Abel's offering, while turning aside Cain's. From Genesis 4:7 it's obvious that God's approval has more to do with Cain's heart than the quality of his physical offering. But the firstborn became terribly angry and, as children will, took it out on his sibling. He killed the approved one, Abel.

What sorrow Eve must have felt. Doubtless, all the

promise she felt at Cain's birth was dimmed. She had lost her younger son, and God had condemned her older one to wander the earth. Yet God renewed his promise by giving Eve a third son, Seth. Of course, no child can take the place of another, but Eve again felt God's love and comfort. And through Seth came the line of salvation, in Noah and his family.

We know no more of Eve's family life than this, but all women can relate to her failings, hurts, and hopes. Just as she is the first woman, from whom all others spring, Eve's life speaks to all of us. Our doubts, sins, and experiences parallel hers. Like her, we may make hasty choices that separate us from God. But like her, we discover that though we desert God, He will not give up on us. He is always calling us back to the garden of His love.

GOMER

When the LORD began to speak through Hosea,
the LORD said to him,
"Go, take to yourself an adulterous wife
and children of unfaithfulness,
because the land is guilty of the vilest adultery
in departing from the LORD."
So he married Gomer daughter of Diblaim,
and she conceived and bore him a son.

HOSEA 1:2–3

Talk about taking your work home with you! That's what
the prophet Hosea did when he married a faithless woman,
Gomer. But God had a plan: He wanted to show Israel
just what their unfaithfulness to Him looked like. So He
gave His people a practical view of it by having the prophet
marry a woman who would seek out other men and bear
illegitimate children.

Gomer's second and third children were probably
those of her lovers, not her husband. Each child had a
name with a meaning. The name of her first son, *Jezreel*,
means "God scatters," a warning to Israel about what
was to come. The first daughter was named *Lo-Ruhamah*
or "not loved." And Lo-Ammi, the last son, has a name
that means "not my people." Sometime following their
birth, Gomer left her husband to live as a prostitute. Her
actions picture the increasing distance between God and
His people. Just as Gomer's sin separated the prophet and

his wife, Israel's worship of pagan gods parted the Lord and His people.

Eventually both Gomer and the Israelites were brought to an impasse. After all her wild living, Gomer ended up a slave. But God commanded the prophet to love her again, so His people who were also about to be enslaved would comprehend how much He loved them. Obedient Hosea bought Gomer back, just as Jesus bought us out of our sin. With great tenderness the prophet returned his wife to her home and commanded her to be faithful.

We cannot know if Gomer appreciated her husband's compassion. Israel did not immediately repent, and perhaps Gomer didn't either. But her fall and reinstatement give today's Christian a clear picture of how much God loves His erring people and the extent He will go to reclaim their love. He does not hold grudges, but calls the wrongdoer to make an about-face and come to Him again.

Have you failed God? He will never fail you. Turn in repentance, and draw near to the One who has never disappointed His beloved. No matter what you've done, He offers forgiveness. Just ask—He's been waiting for you all along.

HAGAR

Now Sarai, Abram's wife,
had borne him no children. . . .
So. . .Sarai his wife took her Egyptian maidservant
Hagar and gave her to her husband to be his wife.
GENESIS 16:1, 3

Perhaps Sarai meant well, but when she tried to generate God's promised child by giving her slave to her husband, she created a relational mess for everyone involved.

Poor Hagar had nothing to say in the situation, and Abram simply went along with his wife's desires. But the plan went miserably awry. As Abram's second wife, Hagar's position became worse, not better. Once she conceived, she despised Sarai and brought trouble down on herself.

Though Sarai had caused the dissension in the family, she blamed Abram for the situation. Abram, who truly loved Sarai and probably simply sought peace in his own tent, left the solution to the problem up to Sarai. She decided to mistreat her slave, so the pregnant Hagar finally fled. Over the desert, she headed for her home in Egypt, though she had little chance of completing the journey.

In the desert, the angel of the Lord appeared to Hagar and turned her back from the dangerous trip, promising she would have a son and that her descendants would be "too numerous to count" (Genesis 16:9). He also prophesied division between Hagar's son, Ishmael, and the child of promise, Isaac.

Fourteen years would pass before Isaac was born, and the division between Sarah, as God had now named her, and Hagar grew even wider. When Ishmael mocked young Isaac, Sarah insisted that her husband, now called Abraham, send the youth away. This time, Abraham went to God, who told him to do as Sarah wished. And once again, God promised that Ishmael would father a nation.

Hagar left with her son. They traveled until they were exhausted, and death from thirst seemed imminent. But God intervened yet again to provide well water. And God continued to watch over Ishmael, who became the father of the Arabs.

The mistreated Hagar seemed deserted as she twice headed off into the desert. But even though she made mistakes and the people around her mistreated her, God never ignored her. At key points, He protected and guided her and her son.

So it can be for us. Life may turn us on our ears, but nothing we experience is beyond God's wisdom or control. With Him, we are always safe, comforted, and protected. He will never leave or forsake us.

HANNAH

[Elkanah] had two wives;
one was called Hannah and the other Peninnah.
Peninnah had children, but Hannah had none.

1 SAMUEL 1:2

Did all the women in the Bible pick on those who couldn't have children? No, not really. But from the biblical record, it seems to have happened often enough. Perhaps God was showing His people why polygamy isn't part of His plan.

Though Hannah's husband, Elkanah, loved her deeply, that only seemed to make her situation worse. Elkanah's second wife, the jealous Penninah, kept picking at the childless favorite until Hannah completely despaired and would not eat.

When they made their annual visit to the tabernacle, Hannah poured out her heart to God. Though she had probably prayed often before this, now she made a special promise: If God would give her a son, she would give the child back to Him to serve Him. She wanted her son to take the Nazirite vow—a sign of special dedication to God—as Samson had.

Even during her heartfelt prayer, more pain came Hannah's way. Eli, the priest, confronted Hannah, accusing her of being drunk. She had to explain that it was her deep need, not wine, that had made her pray silently, yet with her lips moving. The chastened priest believed

Hannah and sent her on her way, blessing her. Then Hannah felt peace in her heart, as her face shone and she ate once again.

Soon, Hannah received the answer to her prayer. She conceived, and in time had a son, whom she named *Samuel*—which means "heard of God." The next year, when her husband wanted her to visit the tabernacle again, she promised to give Samuel to the Lord's service, but not until he was weaned. Since there was no way to keep milk in that era, children were usually weaned around three years old. So Samuel would have had those early years of influence by a godly family, especially his mother. Though Samuel was very young, Hannah must have had a powerful impact upon him, for he became one of Israel's greatest prophets. He led Israel, spiritually, through the important age of the founding of the monarchy.

Hannah kept her promises to her husband and to God. Once Samuel was weaned, she brought him and a generous offering to the tabernacle. After the offering was made, she gave her son to Eli to raise and train in the priesthood.

This amazing woman must have felt sorrow at leaving her child, yet the words from her lips were all praise for the Lord who had brought the situation to pass. She glorified Him for His deliverance, feeling as if she had won the battle with the arrogant Penninah. Her prayer showed deep devotion to God and trust that He was in charge of all that happens on the earth. Perhaps that's why she could leave Samuel with Eli, though his own sons had fallen into wickedness and would be with young Samuel in the tabernacle. She trusted that God would fulfill all she wanted for her son.

Though her contact with Samuel was limited to the annual visit, Hannah faithfully showed him her love, providing him with a gift from home—a robe, which he would have worn every day and remembered her by.

Eli prayed for Hannah and her husband, and they had five more children. The barren woman became fully blessed, because she trusted in God and committed all of her life—even her relationship with her miracle child—to Him.

Isn't Hannah a woman you'd like to meet in heaven? Can't you relate to her on many levels? Her pain has been yours, even if you haven't had trouble conceiving, because relationships are so often complex and hurtful. Like her, you've had to give some treasured things up to God and trust that He would bless you for your sacrifice. You've taken risks for Him and hoped you'd never regret them.

This wonderful mother who almost wasn't one is a beautiful picture for every godly woman today.

HEPHZIBAH

Manasseh was twelve years old when he became king,
and he reigned in Jerusalem fifty-five years.
His mother's name was Hephzibah.

2 KINGS 21:1

"My delight in her" was what Hephzibah's name meant, and though she may have been delightful, her son Manasseh certainly wasn't. Though his father, Hezekiah, sought God and followed him, the boy went the opposite direction, until his name became a byword for evil.

Manasseh returned Israel to pagan worship that was worse than that of the godless nations that previously inhabited the land (see 2 Chronicles 33:9). Only when the Assyrians captured him and brought him to Babylon did the king repent. Though he returned to Jerusalem and reestablished faith in Yahweh, he never successfully wiped out pagan worship practices.

Scripture does not tell us how Hephzibah felt about her son. Perhaps she encouraged him in his wrong practices. Or maybe she wept for his unfaithfulness—and her faithful prayers led to her son's eventual return to God. Either way, her story reminds us that no child is so far away that God cannot reach him. Bringing the lost to Himself is God's plan, even for our own straying children.

HERODIAS

For Herod himself had given orders to have John arrested,
and he had him bound and put in prison.
He did this because of Herodias,
his brother Philip's wife,
whom he had married.

MARK 6:17

As another of the bad babes of the Bible, Herodias had a
checkered career when it came to marriage. She'd married
her uncle, Herod Philip—but when his brother Herod
Antipas visited the couple in Rome, he enticed Herodias
to leave her husband and marry him. Herod Antipas's
position as tetrarch of Galilee and Perea was near that of a
king, so she furthered her own career by going with him.
Seemingly, scripture's condemnation of such a relationship
(see Leviticus 18:16) did not matter.

But when John the Baptist told Herod the marriage
was unlawful, Herodias's marital situation suddenly became
very important. It wasn't that Herodias wanted to do
right—she just wanted to get rid of a critic. But Herod did
not (see Mark 6:19–20).

So the manipulative Herodias had her daughter by her
first husband—not identified in scripture but known to
history as Salome—dance erotically for Herod. Pleased,
Herod offered the girl whatever she wanted. What she
requested was what her mother wanted—John the Baptist's
head.

When people say that how you use your sexuality doesn't matter or that divorce is really okay, remember Herodias. Faithful living before God is built day by day, piece by piece. When we are faithful in the most basic things—like our marriage commitments—we build a good life.

HULDAH

Hilkiah and those the king had sent with him
went to speak to the prophetess Huldah,
who was the wife of Shallum son of Tokhath,
the son of Hasrah, keeper of the wardrobe.
She lived in Jerusalem, in the Second District.

2 CHRONICLES 34:22

When a prophetess spoke, she had to speak the truth—all the time (see Deuteronomy 18:20). And this prophetess did just that, no matter what message God gave her.

As Judah's King Josiah refurbished the temple, his men discovered the Book of the Law. These commands of God had been overlooked for years, when the people of the land had completely fallen into pagan practices.

Confused, the king sent to Huldah to ask what he should do, and she did not withhold the truth. Huldah prophesied that the faithless nation would suffer disaster. But because Josiah had humbly turned to God, it would not occur in his lifetime.

Huldah must have felt compassion for the faithful king

whose people would suffer God's wrath. That didn't change the truth, though, and she spoke the bad news faithfully. But can't you almost hear the gentleness in her voice as she describes God's mercy on the king?

Like Huldah, we need to speak the truth—never harshly but always faithfully. Sometimes we need to bear bad news, but we must also remind people of God's mercy. We are not prophets, but God can use us to speak to others. Are we faithfully portraying His message?

JAEL

Sisera, however, fled on foot to the tent of Jael,
the wife of Heber the Kenite,
because there were friendly relations
between Jabin king of Hazor
and the clan of Heber the Kenite.
JUDGES 4:17

As Israel's commander Barak led his men into battle against the Canaanites, a mysterious woman took a hand in the history of God's people.

The Israelites won the battle. Fleeing on foot, the Canaanite leader Sisera unwittingly leapt from the frying pan into the fire. Jael's husband was a Midianite and had good relations with the Canaanites, so Sisera figured he had found a safe haven when he came to their camp. Perhaps being hidden by a woman seemed particularly safe. Who would barge into her private tent to play "general, general, who's got the general"?

Though Jael hid Sisera in her tent, gave him a drink, and covered him, she had a big surprise for the man. Canaan's commander asked this woman to lie about seeing him, but her only lie was to him. For the bloodthirsty Jael violated her people's laws of hospitality, which required her to protect a guest. Instead, once Sisera fell soundly asleep, Jael used a mallet to drive a tent peg through Sisera's temple.

Interestingly, scripture does not portray Jael as one of the bad babes. Deborah's song of praise pictures her as a heroine (see Judges 5:24–27). Though scripture provides no commentary on Jael's personal morality, Deborah's words approve the salvation she brought to a nation. Surely we must assume God somehow worked in this woman.

Why did Jael suddenly become so vicious? We can only guess. But through her, God fulfilled Deborah's prophecy to the doubting General Barak in Judges 4:9: God handed Sisera over to a woman.

We may ponder Jael's thoughts and actions and wonder what God says through her. But when we look at the larger picture, we can be certain God was in control, protecting His people. Whether Jael was an Israelite who married an unbeliever or whether she was a stranger to God, she became part of His plan.

Just as God acted for Israel's good in the Old Testament, He does so for us today, too. No matter how strange or dangerous our own position, we can be sure God has not left us alone. As we obey Him, He may even use a Jael to bring blessing into our lives. Whenever we entirely trust ourselves to His hands, we are safe.

JAIRUS'S DAUGHTER

Then a man named Jairus,
a ruler of the synagogue,
came and fell at Jesus' feet,
pleading with him to come to his house
because his only daughter,
a girl of about twelve, was dying.
LUKE 8:41–42

A distraught father approached Jesus, begging him to save the life of his young daughter. Though we don't know the girl's name, we can tell how much Jairus loved her. For though he was a leader in his synagogue and Jesus was a controversial figure, this father set aside fear for his position to seek help for his dying daughter.

Jesus agreed to help and turned toward Jairus's house. But at that moment, a woman who had suffered from bleeding all the years Jairus's daughter had lived approached Jesus. She had faith that a simple touch of Jesus' clothing could heal her.

How horrified Jairus must have been when Jesus stopped to heal the woman. Didn't Jesus know Jairus's little girl, the apple of his eye, lay breathing her last breaths?

What a stressful few minutes it must have been for the synagogue ruler. But worse was to come. News arrived that his daughter was dead, the messengers advising Jairus not to "bother" Jesus (see Luke 8:49).

But for Jesus it was no bother. He simply encouraged the synagogue ruler to believe, and moved on. When they reached the house, Jesus immediately calmed the wailing family members, and ignored their mockery when He told them she was "asleep" (Luke 8:52). Then He took the girl's hand and called her to get up. She immediately obeyed, amazing her parents.

What would it have been like to be one of the few people Jesus raised from death? This young girl must always have been special. For the rest of her life, others would have pointed her out because of this event. What importance must she have placed on her own life, knowing God had brought her back from death.

Scripture never says how long or how faithfully this woman lived. Nor does it say how much she appreciated her father's actions on her behalf. But we can assume she never forgot the blessing Jesus gave.

Do we understand how importantly God views each of us? We probably won't be raised physically from the dead—but He has raised us from spiritual death to life in Him. What amazing value our lives must have, if the King of kings died just for us. What more do we need to understand how important we are to Him?

Like this nameless girl, we have been touched by Jesus. Let's live for Him!

JEMIMAH

The first daughter he named Jemimah,
the second Keziah and the third Keren-Happuch.
Nowhere in all the land were there found women
as beautiful as Job's daughters,
and their father granted them an inheritance
along with their brothers.

JOB 42:14–15

Her name meant "daylight," and after the long hard night of suffering her father had, is it any wonder he found joy in her? For Jemimah was the first daughter born after God ended Job's suffering and blessed his life even more than before. Though no child could replace the ones he'd lost, he must have found new delight in Jemimah and her sisters Keziah and Keren-Happuch, along with their seven unnamed brothers.

Since scripture rarely cares much for physical beauty, we can, perhaps, assume that Jemimah also had a spiritual beauty that reflected her father's faith. For how could she have failed to pick up on the joy her father found with God? Job had experienced the Lord's greatness, which must have affected all that he said about God and His blessings.

Whether or not God replaces something we have lost, He can bring us new joy. No matter what our past, we can always delight in the new life He offers day by day.

JEPHTHAH'S DAUGHTER

When Jephthah returned to his home in Mizpah,
who should come out to meet him but his daughter,
dancing to the sound of tambourines!
She was an only child.
Except for her he had neither son nor daughter.
When he saw her, he tore his clothes and cried,
"Oh! My daughter!
You have made me miserable and wretched,
because I have made a vow to
the LORD that I cannot break."

JUDGES 11:34–35

Jephthah made an ill-considered promise to God, one that took the form of a bargain: You bring me home as a victor, and I will make a sacrifice of the first thing that crosses my threshold to greet me.

What was I thinking? he must have asked himself when his daughter danced across the threshold, rejoicing at his return. That thoughtless promise had to be fulfilled at the loss of his only child. His brave daughter agreed to follow through on her father's promise, if for two months she could grieve with her friends in the mountains.

Though the Bible says Jephthah "did to her as he had vowed," interpretations differ as to whether the girl was killed or perhaps given to God in some other fashion— perhaps as a temple servant who would never marry. Either way, Jephthah never delighted in grandchildren.

But his story is a cautionary one. Let us all beware what we promise God, and may we never try to bribe Him with our obedience.

JEZEBEL

> *While Jezebel was killing off the LORD's prophets,*
> *Obadiah had taken a hundred prophets*
> *and hidden them in two caves, fifty in each,*
> *and had supplied them with food and water.*
> 1 KINGS 18:4

If the child Jezebel had gone to school, her report card might have read "Does not play well with others." She is one of the Bible's *really* bad babes, a manipulative woman who just had to have her own way. Ever wonder what a completely conscienceless person looks like? Here she is.

This Sidonian princess married Ahab, king of Israel, and spread the corrupting influence of her pagan gods to the chosen people of the one true God. In the end, Ahab did more to provoke the Lord than all the other kings of Israel who'd gone before him (see 1 Kings 16:33).

Perhaps Jezebel didn't want to hear how bad she was, because she decided to kill off as many of God's prophets as she could (see 1 Kings 18:4). But she didn't catch Elijah. In time, God sent Elijah to the king, to confront Ahab about the pagan priests and prophets imported by Jezebel. The prophet commanded the king to bring the pagan leaders to Mount Carmel, where Elijah proposed a duel between himself and Baal's prophets. They would seek to discover who was more powerful—Baal or God—as the two sides would begin a sacrifice and call on their respective deities to light the fire.

No matter what the Baal worshipers did, their sacrifice would not ignite. Taunting them, Elijah made the challenge harder on himself—and God. He had the Israelites cover his wood with water, jars and jars of it. Then, instead of making a spectacle, he simply prayed. And God's fire fell from heaven, igniting the sacrifice. After that, Israel knew who was really God.

When Jezebel heard what had happened, she wanted to kill Elijah, too. He had to flee, but God protected him from the wicked rulers.

Sometime later, Ahab tried to get a vineyard owner, Naboth, to sell his land to make room for a kingly garden. Naboth rightly refused to give up his inheritance from God. When Jezebel found her husband sulking, she promised to get the land for him—by setting up Naboth. On a day of fasting, she arranged to have two men accuse the honorable Naboth of cursing God and the king. The punishment? Stoning to death. Such an end Naboth suffered, all so Jezebel could get his land for her husband.

Then God sent Elijah to the queen with a message: He confronted her with a murder accusation and promised that where Naboth had died, she would die, too. Worse yet, dogs would eat her body. But not immediately.

When Ahab died in battle against the king of Aram,

Jezebel manipulated her sons, Ahaziah and Joram, who also became kings of Israel. So she remained powerful for about ten years. Her sons were wicked rulers, much like their father.

But Elijah's prophecy did not go unfulfilled. In time, God raised up Jehu to kill off Ahab's line. Jehu killed Joram, who had succeeded to the throne after his brother died from injuries from a fall. Then Jehu, the new king, fulfilled God's prophecy concerning Jezebel—he had her thrown down from her window, where her blood spattered the wall and she was trampled by horses. When servants went to bury her, there was very little left. The men who reported back to the king merely told him of Elijah's prophecy.

"Crime doesn't pay" might be the moral behind Jezebel's life. Her defiance of God got her nowhere. And when she turned to a criminal act, God prepared punishment for her. Though many years passed between Elijah's spoken words and Jezebel's death, God never forgot.

God doesn't forget our deeds, either. When we obey Him, He protects us, as He did Elijah. When we do wrong, we reap a bitter reward.

Are you frustrated by the wicked and powerful? Let's remember we have not read the end of their story. Like Jezebel, they may be storing up disaster for themselves.

JOANNA

Jesus traveled about from one town and village to another,
proclaiming the good news of the kingdom of God.
The Twelve were with him, and also some women
who had been cured of evil spirits and diseases:
Mary (called Magdalene) from whom seven demons
had come out; Joanna the wife of Cuza,
the manager of Herod's household;
Susanna; and many others.
These women were helping to support
them out of their own means.

LUKE 8:1–3

We're left with many questions about Joanna. This passage and Luke 24:10 tell us all we know of her. Though scripture doesn't recount her personal history, we know she was important to Jesus' earthly ministry, since her generous giving helped make it happen.

Some commentators assume Joanna was a widow, since she freely followed Jesus. Cuza would have held an important position in Herod Antipas's household, watching over all the tetrarch's household affairs. If Cuza was still alive, he must have been sympathetic to the gospel, to allow his wife such freedom. Perhaps he was thankful Jesus had healed his wife.

Whatever her marital situation, Joanna provides an excellent example of generous giving. Because she and the other women faithfully continued in this support role, the gospel went out to the world. Do we think our financial support is small or unimportant? Take another look at Joanna and be thankful for the opportunities we have to give.

JOB'S WIFE

His wife said to him,
"Are you still holding on to your integrity?
Curse God and die!"

JOB 2:9

Not exactly the "supportive wife" was Job's mate. The cruelness of these words has forever branded her as an unfeeling woman who could not bear her husband's suffering or trust that God would bring good out of it.

But let's not join Mrs. Job in her insensitivity. Before her stood a man suffering with all of his anatomy—even his breath stank. Her future, along with his, seemed to have landed in a cesspit. She had lost all her children and her hope for future security. Her husband's wealth seemed lost to them. Grief burdened her entire soul.

Since sudden death was seen as punishment for cursing God, Job's wife encouraged him to blaspheme the Lord and end the pain quickly. As she sought a quick way out, Satan used Job's most intimate family member as a tempter. Fortunately, even through his pain, Job understood that taking her advice would only make things worse. He decided his life lay firmly in God's hand—and he would leave it there. Job would not try to manipulate God.

When Job's suffering ends, God blesses him again, making him richer than ever before. The Lord even gives Job ten more children (see Job 42:13). How like God to turn a heart from sorrow to joy, through trust in Him!

Since Job's wife is not directly mentioned again, some have assumed Job's post-trial children to be by another wife. But if Job's first wife was still with him, joy may have filled her heart at her husband's recovery. And God may have blessed her, too, with the thrill of those new lives.

From Job's wife we learn what *not* to do spiritually. Trials and troubles, whether irritating or overwhelming, come to all. From great trials, however, even greater faith may grow—if we don't give in to Mrs. Job's despair.

Look at the wonderful experience Job ultimately had with God. Though his suffering and the incessant blathering of his friends fill most of the book that bears his name, in the end Job understood the priceless depths of God's greatness.

As we deeply trust in God, we follow in Job's footsteps. Clinging to the Lord, we discover nothing can separate us from Him. Holding on to our integrity, we discover God's instead.

JOCHEBED

The name of Amram's wife was Jochebed,
a descendant of Levi,
who was born to the Levites in Egypt.
To Amram she bore Aaron,
Moses and their sister Miriam.
NUMBERS 26:59

Scripture only mentions her by name twice, but through her children we have a clear picture of the kind of mother Jochebed was. Moses became the Old Testament's premier prophet, while Aaron supported him as high priest and Miriam became a prophetess. What a godly influence Jochebed must have been from her children's earliest days.

When Pharaoh declared that all the male Hebrew babies should be killed, Jochebed decided to save Moses. Hiding him as long as possible, she then placed the baby in a rush basket in the Nile River and allowed his sister to hide and watch over him.

How much faith it must have taken for Jochebed to float her son on the river and await his salvation! What fear she must have felt as her baby lay there!

But God's plan was better than Jochebed's wildest dreams: He sent an Egyptian princess to find the boy; Miriam, standing nearby, got to bring her mother to the princess, who made Jochebed the baby's nurse. So the faithful Hebrew mother raised her own child—and obviously trained him in faith. Where else would Moses have gotten His knowledge of the Lord? Certainly not from the pagan priests that filled the Egyptian court.

Jochebed did a good job, too. Moses never forgot her faith lessons, and years later stood up for his enslaved people. When, as a newly called prophet of God, Moses resisted the call, the Lord even provided him with a mouthpiece in his brother, Aaron. Together these boys would do their mama proud, proclaiming God's truth to a whole nation. The books of the Bible penned through Moses begin the Bible's history and tell of God's claims on the lives of believers.

In time, Miriam, too, would join her brothers in a key place of praise and leadership (see Exodus 15:21; Micah 6:4).

When modern society tells you motherhood isn't important, remember Jochebed and her children. The children you tenderly nurture today could tomorrow lead others to Christ through their faithful words and actions. When a woman immerses herself in God, her influence extends around her like ripples in a pool—and who better to be touched by that faith than her children?

JUDITH

When Esau was forty years old,
he married Judith daughter of Beeri the Hittite,
and also Basemath daughter of Elon the Hittite.
They were a source of grief to Isaac and Rebekah.
GENESIS 26:34–35

Esau married late, but the forty years he'd lived didn't bring him wisdom. He wed two women, both of a pagan people. And these marriages must have caused a lot of family strife, since his parents refused to allow their second son, Jacob, to marry a Canaanite (see Genesis 27:46–28:1).

The Canaanite fertility religion, which encouraged prostitution, probably deeply offended Isaac and Rebekah. It certainly wasn't what they had in mind for their eldest son, and perhaps they saw it leading him to disobey God. Since scripture never mentions Judith again, the grief she caused her in-laws is our entire legacy of her.

We, too, may attract the dislike of a prospective in-law. Not everyone will like us—perhaps we'll be criticized because we come from a different ethnicity or because we aren't "important" enough.

But when the critics complain, let it be because we are faithful Christians, not women who lead others astray. Let the slings and arrows fly, but not because we have dishonored God. He's the one we need to please, with our marriages and our lives.

JULIA

Greet Philologus, Julia, Nereus and his sister,
and Olympas and all the saints with them.

ROMANS 16:15

We may not know much about Julia, but the very fact
that Paul greeted her indicates she was a faithful believer.
Will future generations know as much about us? Will they
understand that God applauded us for our faith, as He did
Julia, even if we never get public mention?

This unknown woman was probably a slave or a
former slave who had won her freedom. During the first
century, many masters freed slaves—so many that Rome
actually taxed masters who did so. But a Roman slave
might have had a more secure life than a freedwoman.
At least she would know she had a place to live and food
to keep her alive. Though a freed person had more lib-
erty, security was the price she paid for those greater legal
rights.

If Julia was a slave, perhaps her freedom in Christ com-
forted her. If a freedwoman, perhaps her security lay in
Him. But whatever her condition, she remained true to her
Savior.

May we pass this truth on to future generations, too:
It pays to be faithful to the One who saved us, no matter
what our situation may be.

KETURAH

Abraham took another wife, whose name was Keturah.
She bore him Zimran, Jokshan, Medan,
Midian, Ishbak and Shuah.
GENESIS 25:1–2

Keturah probably wasn't really a "wife"—1 Chronicles
1:32 calls her a concubine. Scholars disagree on when she
entered Abraham's life—some think there was an early
wedding, while others say it happened after Sarah's death.
A third group says there was no wedding at all.

Whatever her legal status, scripture is clear that
Keturah's many children had nothing to do with God's
promise. Though God turned these boys into many
nations, they never held the place of Isaac.

So before his death, Abraham gave gifts to these six
sons and sent them away. Faithful Abraham did not seem
concerned about the anguish that might create for Keturah
or her children. But it had to have created a distressing
situation for everyone.

Like others in the Bible, Keturah and her sons discovered that being out of the center of God's plan can be emotionally painful. We've seen it when friends or family members become romantically involved with non-Christians—
or very unfaithful ones. We've seen it when children walk
away from faith and into trouble.

Relationships that are not in line with God's will generate a lot of hurt, so they all need to be centered in Jesus.

Leaning on Him won't keep us from every problem—but it helps to know He's always right at our side.

LEAH

And Jacob did so.
He finished the week with Leah,
and then Laban gave him his daughter Rachel to be his wife.
GENESIS 29:28

It's hard not to feel sorry for Leah, marrying a man who loved her sister. Her father tricked Jacob, who'd worked seven years for the right to marry his beautiful daughter Rachel. But Laban put his older and plainer daughter, Leah, into Jacob's bed on the wedding night.

How much did Leah know of this plan? Wouldn't she have understood the sorrow that plot would bring to her sister's heart? Was she afraid of her father, an innocent victim of his conniving, or an eager part of the plan? We don't know. But the situation Laban instigated made his daughters' family life incredibly complex and agonizing.

To "solve" this marital problem, Laban suggested that Jacob marry Rachel, in exchange for an additional seven years of work. Both daughters must have felt manipulated by their father, who clearly wanted to keep a good worker at the expense of his own children's happiness.

Jacob loved Rachel, and everyone in the camp must have known it. But God had compassion on the unloved

Leah and gave her children, while withholding babies from Rachel. Though Rachel received her husband's love, God gave two very special things to Leah—Israel's priestly line came from her third son, Levi, and the Messiah's ancestry from her fourth son, Judah.

Unfortunately, Leah believed that having babies was the way to win her husband's heart—and Rachel became so jealous of her sister's fertility that she started a personal version of "can you top this?" that made everyone in the family miserable. Rachel told Jacob to take her maid, Bilhah, as a concubine, to bear sons in her place. Leah immediately retaliated by giving her maid, Zilpah, to Jacob, too. Bilhah had two sons, and Rachel felt she had won. Then Zilpah bore Gad and Asher, and Leah rejoiced.

One day, Leah's first son, Reuben, found some mandrake roots, which were superstitiously believed to affect fertility. Desperate Rachel begged her sister for them, and the depth of Leah's pain is clear in her mournful answer: "Wasn't it enough that you took away my husband? Will you take my son's mandrakes too?" (Genesis 30:15).

In return for the mandrakes, Rachel offered Leah the chance to sleep with their husband. Leah agreed, and again became pregnant. She had two more children before God gave Rachel her first son, Joseph.

When God told Jacob to return to his homeland, Leah and Rachel didn't object—probably because Laban hadn't been such a wonderful father. They slipped off, with all the flocks Jacob had received from his father-in-law, while Laban was away.

Only once more would Leah see her father, when he followed the fleeing family—not from concern for his children but to seek out some missing idols. He didn't even try to lay claim to his daughters or their children, though he finally created a covenant between himself and his son-in-law that considered his children's welfare.

Later, when Jacob faced his cheated brother Esau, whose anger he feared, he made it clear which wife was most important: Leah was placed nearer to danger than Rachel. How that must have pained Leah! But more pain was coming. On the trip to Jacob's home, Leah's daughter, Dinah, was raped by a local prince. It seemed as if anguish was Leah's lot.

Leah may have been the most unloved woman of the Bible. Through no fault of her own, she never had her husband's affection—only his children. Nor did her conniving father care for her. But Leah shows us what God can do, even with a hurting heart. Though she didn't have anything approximating a perfect life, God blessed her in ways that escaped the more-loved Rachel.

God can also take our less-than-perfect lives and make them perfect in Him. We may never get all the human love and attention we'd like to have, but He'll always draw us near His side. And isn't that where we really want to be anyway?

LOIS

I have been reminded of your sincere faith,
which first lived in your grandmother Lois
and in your mother Eunice and,
I am persuaded, now lives in you also.

2 TIMOTHY 1:5

When she first believed, Lois probably never thought she was starting a spiritual legacy. But she passed her faith on to her daughter, Eunice. As they went about their daily lives, these two women powerfully impacted the man whom the apostle Paul would see as surrogate son and a partner in spreading the gospel. To young Timothy, Paul passed on an important ministry that has touched believers around the world.

Ever feel as if you're "only a mother"? Yours is an important role that influences lives. Someday you may be a grandmother, too. How many young people could be touched by your faithful example, years in the making? Lois probably never thought her faith legacy would be reported twenty centuries later. But Paul's letters to her grandson still guide Christians today.

Gomer conceived again and gave birth to a daughter.
Then the LORD said to Hosea, "Call her Lo-Ruhamah,
for I will no longer show love to the house of Israel,
that I should at all forgive them."

HOSEA 1:6

Imagine being named "not loved." How devastating it must have been for this child to know that God was using her as an example to her people—an example of the results of their sin. God had set the nation aside because of its unbelief, and Lo-Ruhamah's mother, Gomer, had acted out on that lack of faith. Her daughter probably wasn't even Hosea's child.

No matter how well Hosea treated her, that knowledge must have marred this child's life. But just as God wooed His people back to Himself, perhaps He called Lo-Ruhamah to Himself. For even when God declares their sin to His people, it is only to separate them from the wrong and bring them into relationship with Him.

As God called His ancient people away from their transgressions and into His love, He calls us. Are we trapped in sin? He will cleanse us from it. Do we crave love? He provides all we need. None of us must remain unloved. We need only to seek Jesus with all our hearts—and we will find Him.

LOT'S WIFE

But Lot's wife looked back,
and she became a pillar of salt.
GENESIS 19:26

Angels rescued Lot's family from the destruction that fell on the city of Sodom. The city was so evil that God saved only Abraham's nephew and his immediate family. Physically pulling Lot's family from Sodom, the heavenly beings warned the humans not to look back.

What a temptation it must have been to look over a shoulder and see the horrifying events. Didn't each person wonder what had happened to the friends and family members there—especially the daughters' fiancés who would not come with them? But only Lot's wife gave in to the temptation. And she lost her life, turning into a pillar of salt.

On top of all the mayhem and destruction, how awful that must have been for Lot's family. But it showed them—and us today—that disobedience of God's express commands comes at a very high cost. We may never become salt monoliths, but how does sin impact our lives?

Can we look back at damage sin has caused? Or sin confessed that still calls our names? Or wrong choices we've repented of that still haunt us? God doesn't want that backward glance to destroy us. We live in Him today—so let's peer forward at the goals He's set before us.

LYDIA

One of those listening was a woman named Lydia,
a dealer in purple cloth from the city of Thyatira,
who was a worshiper of God.
The Lord opened her heart to respond to Paul's message.
When she and the members of her household were baptized,
she invited us to her home.
"If you consider me a believer in the Lord," she said,
"come and stay at my house." And she persuaded us.
ACTS 16:14–15

The first person to be baptized on European soil was Lydia, a prosperous merchant. A "seller of purple," she either sold purple dye or the fabric it tinted. You might call Lydia a first-century businesswoman.

But she wasn't just about business. Lydia listened carefully to Paul, and God opened her heart in faith to receive Jesus as Savior. Quickly, she acted on her faith and invited Paul, Silas, and Timothy to her home. Later, after Paul and Silas were briefly imprisoned on flimsy charges, she did not fail to welcome them to come again to her home.

What an example of immediate, purposeful faith Lydia is for us. Do we move forward in the right direction, or hold back, waiting until we see if our choices will be popular? Lydia set her sights on doing God's will and carried on. Do we?

MAHLAH

*Now Zelophehad. . .had no sons but only daughters,
whose names were Mahlah, Noah,
Hoglah, Milcah and Tirzah.
They went to Eleazar the priest, Joshua son of Nun,
and the leaders and said,
"The LORD commanded Moses to give us
an inheritance among our brothers."
So Joshua gave them an inheritance along with the brothers
of their father, according to the LORD's command.*
JOSHUA 17:3–4

You might say the leaders of Israel appreciated women's
rights. At least, following Moses' former decision (see
Numbers 27:1–7), they confirmed the rights of women to
inherit when there were no sons who could. How much
safer Mahlah and her sisters must have felt, knowing they
would never be left poverty-stricken.

But Numbers 36 tells us more of these women. The men
of their clan became worried that their lands would pass into
other tribes of Israel, once the women married. So God commanded that these ladies marry within their own tribe.

But think about it: Hadn't God already planned their
weddings, even from the moment He told Moses they
could inherit? Every detail of a believer's life is thought out
beforehand by our glorious Lord. All things work together
for good—and for God, when we walk faithfully in our
Master's way.

MARTHA

As Jesus and his disciples were on their way,
he came to a village where a woman
named Martha opened her home to him.
LUKE 10:38

Martha was a warmhearted woman. We know that because she invited Jesus and His disciples to visit, even though that would be a lot of trouble. After all, feeding such a crowd on short notice wasn't the easiest thing in the days before refrigerators, microwaves, and gas or electric ovens.

It didn't matter that she and her family were probably well-to-do. That just meant Martha had to organize her staff, perhaps bring on some temporary help, and get everyone to work quickly at the last minute to feed over a dozen houseguests. But that major challenge didn't stop Martha from being generous.

Perhaps the honor of having Jesus in her home made Martha want to excel in her entertaining. It had to be a real Martha Stewart event in His honor. But while she worried if the centerpiece would be just perfect, directed the servants, and debated with herself if she'd have enough food, she missed out on an important event: Jesus was teaching in her own home, and she didn't hear a word.

Finally, irked that her sister Mary wasn't helping, Martha asked Jesus to intercede and make Mary lend a hand. What a shock it must have been when the Master took her sister's side! The kingdom of God was more important than a single meal, as Jesus gently told Martha.

Despite Jesus' rebuke, this dinner helped cement a strong relationship between the family and Jesus, for when Martha and Mary's brother, Lazarus, fell ill, they sent directly for Him with the message, "The one you love is sick" (John 11:3). Martha and her sister obviously expected that, at the news, Jesus would come running to heal their brother. After all, hadn't He done that for many in Israel? Though they waited, Jesus did not come—and time ran out for Lazarus.

John 11:5 tells us that Jesus loved the family, yet he intentionally waited, knowing the wonderful miracle He would perform in a few days. For Martha and Mary, those days were agony. Four days after their brother's death, Jesus appeared.

" 'Lord,' Martha said to Jesus, 'if you had been here, my brother would not have died. But I know that even now God will give you whatever you ask' " (John 11:21–22). Such freedom of speaking shows that Martha's relationship to Jesus had remained close, in spite of His earlier rebuke. Despite the awful situation, as her brother's body began to decay, Martha's faith that Jesus could still help her remained strong.

Jesus responded vaguely, speaking about the resurrection. Martha had no doubt that her brother would be with God at the last day, but she was more interested in this day than the last one.

Jesus encouraged her to faith, and her response, "Yes, Lord. . .I believe that you are the Christ, the Son of God, who was to come into the world" (John 11:27), shows her understanding of who He was—and is.

But what a huge shock it still must have been when Jesus raised her brother from the dead. Rejoicing mingled with amazement. Jesus had done just what she'd asked, and as a result, He'd performed a miracle that would set all Israel on its ear!

Many of us can see ourselves in Martha. We have a great desire to serve God, and we open ourselves to service—then get bogged down in the little things that don't mean much to ministry. With this well-meaning woman, God shows us where the important things are—in our relationship with Christ, not the busyness of doing things for Him.

Obviously Martha learned her lesson. When her brother became ill, she focused on the important things. And her relationship with Jesus had become one of deep trust. She did not fear asking Him for the one thing she really needed—the return of her brother to earthly life. And Jesus gave her just that.

Are we afraid to ask Him for what we really need? Perhaps that's the only thing He's waiting for. It's a technique Martha would recommend.

MARY MAGDALENE

*Jesus traveled about from one town and village to another,
proclaiming the good news of the kingdom of God.
The Twelve were with him, and also some
women who had been cured of evil spirits
and diseases: Mary (called Magdalene)
from whom seven demons had come out. . . .*

LUKE 8:1–2

How embarrassed and even angry Mary of Magdala might
feel if she were with us today. She suffers from a terrible
reputation, even though scripture gives us no reason to
believe it.

All we know of her background is that, once Mary
Magdalene had been healed of a horrible demon infesta-
tion, she followed Jesus faithfully, helping support the
ministry out of her own money (see verse 3). But somehow, perhaps because of her unusual demon possession or
because of the story that comes shortly before the mention
of her name, people have erroneously connected her to
Luke 7:36–50, which tells of the prostitute who washed
Jesus' feet with perfume.

Until Jesus came along, how this woman suffered, in
torment from evil spirits that probably influenced her body,
mind, and spirit. Though she may have been somewhat
well-to-do (since she could afford to support Jesus' ministry), what did that money mean if no one could heal her?
How welcome the relief of Jesus' touch on her life. She had

great reason to feel deep devotion toward her Savior.

Since Mary's name appears at the head of lists of the women she associates with, perhaps she had more stature than the others. Whatever her position in society, she has an important role in scripture. She was there, among a small coterie of women, when Jesus was crucified (see Matthew 27:56). She was the first to see the resurrected Jesus, and since John tells the women's story from her point of view, the disciple must have relied heavily on her recounting of events when he wrote his Gospel (see John 20:1–18). And the other women mentioned in Matthew 28:1, Mark 16:1, and Luke 24:10 certainly backed up her description of the events.

On that Sunday after Jesus' death, while the male disciples were still in bed or perhaps hiding from the Roman authorities, the women went to the gravesite to prepare the body. Now that the Sabbath was ended, they could complete Friday's hurriedly performed task (see Mark 16:1).

What a surprise awaited them at the tomb: There was no body! Though the women had followed Him faithfully and listened to His preaching, this was beyond their expectations. At the command of the angels they met at the tomb, the women ran to get the disciples Peter and John, who could hardly believe their tale—but came to see for themselves.

Once the disciples had left, the most amazing thing happened. Two angels appeared to Mary Magdalene, sitting where Jesus had been laid. They asked why she cried, and she replied that someone had taken her Lord away.

Turning, she saw, but did not recognize, Jesus Himself. When He asked why she cried and what she looked for, she demanded to know where Jesus' body had been taken. But as soon as He spoke her name, Mary recognized Him. Jesus sent her to the disciples again, bearing the joyful news.

Appreciative of the work Jesus had done in her life, Mary spent the rest of her life in His service. Whether she followed Him during His ministry or ran to tell the confused disciples of her experience, Mary always had Jesus at the center of her existence. While others slept, she wanted to care for His body. Is it any wonder that Jesus appeared first to this faithful woman?

Do we constantly seek Jesus in our lives, too? Or does He live on a back shelf, to be trotted out when we feel we have time for Him? Like Mary, we are blessed when we make Him the focus of our being. As we are increasingly obedient, we'll be amazed at the way He uses us to minister to others.

MARY OF BETHANY

And after she had said this,
she went back and called her sister Mary aside.
"The Teacher is here," she said, "and is asking for you."
When Mary heard this, she got up quickly and went to him.
JOHN 11:28–29

Mary is the sister who chose "what is better" (Luke 10:42).
While her sister, Martha, saw to making a special din-
ner, Mary relaxed at Jesus' feet and listened to Him speak.
While Martha saw to bodies being fed, Mary's soul received
sustenance. Though a meal would be consumed in an hour,
Mary's food lasted for eternity.

Martha was a faithful woman, but Mary may just have
had that extra devotion that sets some people apart. While
others easily became distracted, she only had eyes for Jesus.

Scholars suspect that Martha was a widow, with a house
in which her younger siblings lived with her. It would be
natural, then, for her to see to the arrangements for dinner.
One could understand, though, if she had given directions
to her servants, then returned to Jesus to hear His words.
But foolish household cares distracted the older sister while
the younger one made a wiser choice.

The next time we meet these sisters, their brother
has died. Though Jesus loved Lazarus deeply, He did not
respond to a call for help from Mary and Martha until
Lazarus had been in the grave for four days. As Lazarus lay
dying, how the sisters must have wished for Jesus' presence.

When He came, they both said mournfully, "Lord, if you had been here, my brother would not have died" (see John 11:21, 32).

But it wasn't that Jesus was insensitive to the women and their brother. When Mary spoke, He was troubled. He understood the pain of death in human lives, and on His way to the tomb, the Savior wept.

What joy must have filled Mary's heart to have her brother returned to life by Jesus. Though decay had started to destroy Lazarus, Mary's Savior restored every cell in her brother's body and returned his spirit to it.

Because many believed in Him that day, the jealous Jewish leaders plotted to take Jesus' life. And in the way the Spirit often works, Mary was later inspired to do something to help people understand that the Savior came to die.

Six days before the Passover, as Jesus passed through Bethany on his way to Jerusalem, Mary did something extraordinary that is recorded in three gospels (Matthew 26:6–13; Mark 14:3–9; John 12:1–8). While He dined at the home of Simon the Leper, Mary came to Him with a fine alabaster jar containing pure nard, a very expensive perfume. As was the custom in that day, she anointed Christ with the perfume, pouring it over his head and feet.

In doing this, Mary had taken the task of a servant. Buying a costly perfume, waiting on Jesus herself, and wiping His feet with her hair all showed her humility. In Mary's day, a woman of her position would not unbind her hair in public. But she was so caught up in her devotion that even that did not seem too much. She was totally empowered by love.

When Judas tried to pour cold water on the beautiful act, complaining that the money spent on the perfume could have done much to help the poor, Jesus stood up for Mary and connected her service to His coming death.

Every Christian woman asks herself if she's a Mary or a Martha. The truth is probably somewhere in the middle. It wasn't that Martha didn't love Jesus. She just needed a course correction when she got caught up in less important things. Sometimes we do that, too. But Mary reminds us that a clean house and chef-quality food are less important than our relationships, especially our relationship with Jesus.

Are we settling for the good things of this world and ignoring more valuable spiritual matters? If we're not building our relationship with Jesus, perhaps we've turned into Marthas who need to walk on Mary's side for a while.

MARY, THE MOTHER OF JESUS

But the angel said to her,
"Do not be afraid, Mary, you have found favor with God.
You will be with child and give birth to a son,
and you are to give him the name Jesus."
LUKE 1:30–31

Mary is surely the best-known woman of the Bible. She got to do something no one else could—bear and raise God's Son, Jesus.

This young peasant girl was engaged to Joseph when an angel appeared to say she would bear the Messiah. Shocked, but still showing faith, she asked, "How will this be. . .since I am a virgin?" (Luke 1:34). Though the angel's news must have troubled her, she quickly responded, "I am the Lord's servant. . . . May it be to me as you have said" (Luke 1:38).

What questions surely filled her mind. How would she explain this to Joseph? What would the neighbors think? How would her life change?

But Mary's heart was true to God, and she accepted His glorious mission—the most intimate mission a woman could have. Her sacrifice of body and soul is unparalleled in human history.

God immediately gave Mary encouragement through her cousin Elizabeth, who was pregnant with John the Baptist. When Elizabeth confirmed what the angel had said, Mary praised God for His great blessing. Indeed,

God blessed every aspect of her life as He worked out all things for the mother of His child—from the explanation to Joseph through the birth and all the troubles that followed. All her life, Mary clung to the truths of those days, which would guide her faith.

What work and delight it must have been to raise the Savior! But we know little of this time. The only mention of Jesus' early days, following His birth and circumcision, comes in Luke 2:41–52, when Mary and Joseph lost the twelve-year-old at the temple. The couple didn't always understand this divine Son, but they raised Him faithfully.

Mary became part of Christ's first miracle at the wedding in Cana, for she pointed out the need and told the servants to follow His commands. But from that point on, God's Son pursued His holy mission, and Mary is rarely mentioned. We can guess the anguish she must have felt as she heard of the religious leaders' disapproval of Jesus. What this peasant woman understood, at least in part, these powerful men had no inkling of: God's Son stood before them.

As Jesus' ministry grew, Mary and her other children went to Him to make Him rest from it (see Matthew 12:46–50; Mark 3:31–35; Luke 8:19–21). Jesus' choice to hold fast to God's will for Him, rather than clinging to family ties, must have concerned His mother.

At the foot of the cross, Mary appears again. At His first visit to the temple, the prophet Simeon had prophesied that a sword would pierce Mary's soul (see Luke 2:35). Watching Jesus' death undoubtedly wounded her like nothing else could, for she had given Him His earthly birth. But even from the cross, Jesus watched over Mary and placed her in the care of His disciple John. She went to live with him.

Mary's final appearance is found in Acts 1:14, in the upper room with the disciples and her other sons. Though she surely had many questions along the way, and though Jesus' half brothers must have wondered at much that He did, in our last glimpse of Mary and her family, they are united in the church.

Mary had no easy life. She was not born into wealth, as one might have expected of the woman chosen to bear God's child. Her reputation was destroyed by the unusual circumstances of her first child's birth. But through it all, she pondered the revelation she had been given and continued to trust in God. And He never forsook her.

What a wonderful example Mary is to us. Do we give ourselves completely to our Lord—body, soul, and spirit? Or do we hold back when He asks something that seems "unreasonable"? Mary didn't. Though she obviously had her doubts, she remained true to God's calling for her life. Mary stood firm during pain, doubt, and fear. Will we do less?

MICHAL

Now Saul's daughter Michal was in love with David,
and when they told Saul about it,
he was pleased.
1 SAMUEL 18:20

While David was still pretty much a nobody, Michal fell in love with him. Because of David's successes, her father, King Saul, had given him a high position in the army. But when this new commander won victory and the people's acclaim, the king became jealous. To bind David to himself, Saul offered marriage to his eldest daughter, Merab. But Saul didn't keep the promise, and she married another man.

Now, hearing that Michal loved David, the crafty Saul decided to use her to entrap the popular young man. He sent David out to battle, after telling his prospective son-in-law that the price of the marriage was to be one hundred foreskins from Philistine warriors. Saul figured the Philistines could take care of this thorn in his side by killing David off.

But God defended David, who came home with twice the number of foreskins required. Saul had no choice but to marry off Michal to David. Realizing that God was favoring David, King Saul feared his son-in-law even more—so he again plotted the younger man's death. But Saul made a mistake in telling his son Jonathan of the plan. Jonathan loved David and warned him.

In the grip of an evil spirit, Saul tried to kill David himself, flinging a spear in his direction while his son-in-law played the harp. Following David's escape, Saul sent men to watch his house.

Michal warned David that her father would kill him the next day and helped her husband escape through a window. Then she placed an idol in his bed, covering it to make it look like the sleeping David. When Saul's men came after her husband, she lied, saying David was ill. Cornered in her deceit by her angry father, Michal again lied, saying she let David go so he wouldn't kill her.

Saul continued to harass David, and had Michal married to another man, Paltiel, son of Laish (see 1 Samuel 25:44). Scripture doesn't say whether Michal objected to the change in husband. As long as Saul was powerful, she remained Paltiel's wife. But David gained strength, and when Abner, Saul's commander-in-chief, went over to his side, David demanded that Abner bring him Michal. Though her second husband came weeping behind her, she was forcefully carried to David. Had her love for David died or was she just tired of being a political pawn? The Bible never tells us.

Having Saul's daughter as his wife secured his political position, and David became king of all Israel. But perhaps his high-handed attitude had damaged the relationship with Michal. When he came into Jerusalem, bringing the ark of the covenant back, David danced before it. Michal watched from a window, not rejoicing at the return of the ark, but despising her husband. When he returned to the palace, she met him on the doorstep, criticizing his supposedly undignified actions. Offended, David told her he was celebrating before God and would be even more undignified, if that is what it meant to worship the Lord. We can surmise that the virile David had nothing to do with Michal after that, for she never had children.

Michal had a sad life. Her father and David used her to gain their own ends. Obviously she wasn't Suzie Sunshine either, since she lied easily to her father and had an idol handy to slip into David's bed. But we can't blame her for disliking her treatment as a pawn in the political game.

Michal's personal woes stemmed from her confused marital status. Let us remember that God takes marriage very seriously: It pictures His relationship with us and cannot be put on and taken off at will. Those who forget that may find their relationships unnecessarily tangled. Lifelong faithfulness to a loving husband pays a real bonus in later success.

MIRIAM

Then Miriam the prophetess, Aaron's sister,
took a tambourine in her hand,
and all the women followed her,
with tambourines and dancing.

EXODUS 15:20

Though she had an important task, Miriam is not named in the scriptures' first reference to her. Exodus 2:3–4 simply tells us that Jochebed placed her son Moses in a basket and allowed her daughter to watch over him.

Can there be any doubt that Jochebed had carefully instructed her daughter in what to do? But it was still a hard task. As young Miriam guarded her brother, did she begin to get bored, or did fear keep her on edge? How long did it take for the princess to find Moses? Yet Miriam waited. This brave child took on the job her mother assigned her and did it to perfection.

Once her brother had been found, Miriam, who'd watched from a distance, came forward and asked the Egyptian princess if she'd like her to find a nurse for the child. Could the princess have expected anyone but the boy's mother? Yet even though she knew the babe had to be a Hebrew, the princess did not use that information against Miriam or her mother. Brave though she'd been, how grateful Miriam must have been that there was no trouble and that her younger brother would be safe.

Many years later, we briefly meet Miriam as a worship

leader, following the Hebrews' successful crossing of the Red Sea. And Exodus 15:20 describes Miriam as a prophetess. Though her brothers held the positions of foremost prophet and priest, she had an important role, too, in her peoples' faith life. God had given her a great gift to use for their benefit.

But when God gave seventy elders the gift of prophecy, Miriam and her brother Aaron became jealous of Moses' special relationship with God. Perhaps they felt their positions had been lessened. So, like many people, they picked an argument on a minor point—Moses' marriage to a Cushite. Whether this was Zipporah or a second wife is unclear, but the situation caused trouble for their brother. Still, the meek Moses did not react in anger—God did. Before Moses, He confronted Miriam and Aaron with their sin. Why, He asked, weren't they afraid to do this to Moses, before whom He spoke face-to-face? Then suddenly, God left them.

As the brothers turned and looked at Miriam, they must have been amazed and terrified. She stood before them as a leper, her skin white. Immediately, Aaron repented and asked that Moses bring her healing. So Moses called out to God. The Lord commanded that for a week Miriam should be confined outside the camp, as one who was unclean. Since Miriam was brought back into the camp, we know she had been healed both physically and spiritually. For no one with leprosy would have been allowed back in the community, and God's healings always affect the spirit as well as the body.

Since she was the one punished, Miriam probably started this trouble—but it must not have been her usual sort of action, if the love with which her brothers immediately responded tells us anything. Aaron confessed their mutual sin and sought her healing. Moses quickly turned to God, showering his own forgiveness on his sister. Perhaps the prophet remembered that as a child, without her help, he might not have lived.

Miriam died in Kadesh, according to Numbers 20:1, and was buried there.

She was a God-gifted leader who held an important position in her nation and must have strongly led her people in belief—though she was far from perfect. God gave Miriam a place of authority, and she misused it for a short time. Her punishment was also short-term, so she must have learned her lesson.

If we are in positions of leadership, we also may fail. Let us not judge Miriam, but learn from her mistake. Many years of faithfulness do not armor us against sin. Every day the evil one tempts us. Only constant watchfulness keeps him from our door. Yet when we draw close to Jesus, we can live faithfully for Him.

*Now two prostitutes came to the king
and stood before him.
One of them said, "My lord,
this woman and I live in the same house.
I had a baby while she was there with me.
The third day after my child was born,
this woman also had a baby. We were alone;
there was no one in the house but the two of us.
During the night this woman's son died
because she lay on him."*

1 KINGS 3:16–19

These women hadn't chosen wisely in their profession, and they weren't the kind of folks faithful Jews wanted to be around. But somehow their case landed in the king's court, perhaps because it was such a difficult decision. In a short time, each of the women had birthed a child. But one morning one babe was dead, and both women claimed theirs was the living child.

In God's wisdom Solomon called for a sword and offered to solve the problem by dividing the single baby between them. One mother cried out to give the child to the other, so the king awarded her the child. Such love identified the loving mother, who deserved to have a child in her care. But along with Solomon's court, she undoubtedly was stunned at the king's ability to discern the truth.

Have you ever been surprised at the way God's truth

works in your life? When things seem at their lowest, He quietly intervenes, and life is changed. Suddenly that thorny problem is solved by a knowledge beyond anything you possess.

NAAMAN'S SERVANT GIRL

Now bands from Aram had gone out
and had taken captive a young girl from Israel,
and she served Naaman's wife. She said to her mistress,
"If only my master would see the prophet who is in Samaria!
He would cure him of his leprosy."
2 Kings 5:2–3

This nameless servant had been torn from her home and all that was familiar by a marauding band of Arameans. Now, she was the servant of the commander in chief of the army.

But no one had torn her from her faith. Perhaps her master and mistress were kind to her, for when she saw the man's hurt, she had a good idea: Naaman should go to Elisha the prophet and seek healing.

Desperate, Naaman decided to take her advice. He got an introductory letter from the king of Aram, written to Israel's king, and a carried with him a small fortune in gifts. When he received the letter, King Joram of Israel feared the Arameans were actually trying to provoke a war. But Elisha demanded to have the man sent to him. By his actions the prophet would prove the power of God to this foreigner.

Proud Naaman went to Elisha, expecting to be treated like an important person. But the prophet thought humility would better serve this powerful man. So he did not meet him but sent a message: Wash seven times in the Jordan River.

At first, Naaman refused, angered that the prophet had not treated him as he would have expected. Naaman was even insulted that the rivers in his own land were not deemed good enough. It took some humble people—his servants—to convince Naaman that he risked remaining a leper, when he could be made whole. Once the commander obeyed Elisha, he was healed entirely, both physically and spiritually. Naaman returned and confessed his faith to Elisha, wanting to follow God in his own land.

Though the servant girl had lost her home and freedom, she remained a witness for God. Through her simple suggestion a leader of the Arameans came to the Lord. Who knows what kind of witness he became?

Are we witnesses in the simple things of everyday life? Or are our mouths closed by doubt and fear? Like the unimportant servant girl, we need to do God's will wherever we are. Let's not be deterred by our place in life, our enemies, or anything else. God uses the most amazing people to serve Him well.

NAOMI

Then Naomi said to her two daughters-in-law,
"Go back, each of you, to your mother's home.
May the LORD show kindness to you,
as you have shown to your dead and to me.
May the LORD grant that each of you will find rest
in the home of another husband."
Then she kissed them and they wept aloud.
RUTH 1:8–9

Naomi had fallen on hard times—in a strange land. Famine had caused her and her family to move to Moab. Then her husband and sons died, leaving her with only two daughters-in-law. How could three women make it in a world where women didn't exactly have career options?

Naomi selflessly decided to send the younger women back to their own homeland, where they were more likely to find new husbands. You might say she encouraged them in the best career choice for women of that day.

One of the women, Orpah, took Naomi's suggestion. Perhaps she did find a fine husband, but scripture doesn't say. As she walked out of Naomi's life, she exited the biblical record.

But Ruth clung to Naomi and refused to leave. Maybe she had seen something in her husband's faith that she didn't want to lose. Perhaps she believed in God and felt bound to her mother-in-law. Whatever the reason, the two returned to Naomi's homeland at Bethlehem. When her friends recognized her, Naomi told them not to call her by her name, which means "pleasant," but to call her *Mara*, which translates as "bitter." Grief had overwhelmed Naomi's gentle heart to the point that she felt afflicted by God.

Instead of following their traditional right and leaning on a man of Naomi's extended family, the destitute women fended for themselves. During harvesttime, the law commanded landowners not to take in every bit of the crop (see Leviticus 23:22). They were to leave some grain at the edges, to provide for the poor and the alien. So poor and alien Ruth volunteered to gather barley for herself and her mother-in-law.

But God had a better plan. In one of those divine "coincidences," Ruth found herself gleaning the fields of Boaz, a wealthy man distantly related to Naomi's husband. Boaz had heard reports of Ruth's industry and her care for her mother-in-law, so he commanded his workers to leave her a little extra grain and look after her the whole day. Boaz made it his job to protect this foreign woman who understood the requirements of God's servant.

That evening, as Ruth told Naomi about her day, the older woman recognized Boaz as one of their kinsman-redeemers—a man who could be called on to rescue them in need. As the harvest ended, Naomi decided to help romance out a bit, by placing Ruth in Boaz's path.

Naomi sent her daughter-in-law to Boaz, during the threshing time with a plan: Ruth was to tell Boaz of his responsibility to help them. And help them this generous man did. After looking into their legal situation, he took responsibility for the women, though he was not their closest kinsman-redeemer. Perhaps because he admired her so, he married Ruth and also provided for Naomi.

Following the command of Deuteronomy 25:5–6, Ruth's first child, Obed, became the heir to Ruth's first husband. So Naomi's sorrow turned to joy, and she was not left destitute her in her old age. God provided for her through another generation.

Though Naomi had hard times, God looked after her. Ruth may have seemed an unlikely supporter, but she was faithful—and, through God's blessing, provided well for both of them.

Over time, have things so changed that our Lord no longer cares for His people? No! He never promises lives of ease, just that He will take care of us. Though our life roads may take unexpected turns, we cannot go anywhere that He cannot reach us.

We may feel discouraged, but we must not give up. Who knows when a Ruth or Boaz will enter our lives and do wonderful things for us? There will always be a kinsman-redeemer. God never forgets any of His children—He saves every one.

*And Noah and his sons and his wife and his sons' wives
entered the ark to escape the waters of the flood.*
GENESIS 7:7

God came to Noah with a mission of salvation: Build an
ark, bring in the animals and your family, and be saved.

You have to wonder how Mrs. Noah heard about her
husband's future plans. Over breakfast one morning did
he say, "Oh, by the way, God says I should build an ark,
because there's going to be a flood"? Maybe his wife wondered what practical experience her husband had that would
make him good at boat-building. And what was a flood
anyway?

Did Noah's neighbors make fun of him for his ark-
building project? Maybe so—but as far as we know, his
wife never discouraged him from continuing. Perhaps she
trusted her husband because she'd seen evidence of the wisdom his faith brought him. Maybe she walked closely with
God, too.

Whether or not she'd chosen it, Mrs. Noah became
part of Noah's salvation mission. She had to live on the
ark for many months, smelling the terrible odors the animals put off and trying to keep "house" in impossible
circumstances. There must have been times when she
wondered how she got into this—and what was going to
become of her family. Stress-free living certainly wasn't
part of the ark experience.

Yet the day came when God commanded everyone to come out of the ark. Noah prepared a sacrifice, and God promised such destruction would never again happen. He blessed the members of Noah's family and commanded them to multiply and cover the earth. What joy must have filled the earth as the animals headed off to their favorite watering holes, caves, and other spots.

Sometimes, like Mrs. Noah, we end up part of a mission that doesn't have our names on it. When a husband takes on a role in church leadership, it impacts his wife, too. When a church decides to open a new ministry, we may find ourselves drafted into an unexpected position. How do we respond? Are we good-natured supporters, or do we start whining and complaining? Complaints never glorify God, but willing service—like Mrs. Noah's—always will.

ORPAH

At this they wept again.
Then Orpah kissed her mother-in-law good-by,
but Ruth clung to her.
RUTH 1:14

Orpah will always be known as the woman who left her mother-in-law when times were hard. But to do Orpah justice, she made what she thought was the best decision in the midst of a heartbreaking situation.

After Naomi's husband and two sons died, her daughters-in-law, Orpah and Ruth, began to accompany Naomi on her journey back to Israel. But when they set out on the road that would lead them back to the land of Judah, Naomi began to have second thoughts. She told her daughters-in-law, "Go back, each of you, to your mother's home. . . . May the LORD grant that each of you will find rest in the home of another husband" (Ruth 1:8–9). After all, Orpah and Ruth were not Israelites, and Naomi didn't know what would happen when she returned to her own land. The two younger women probably had a more secure future in their own country of Moab, where they could marry more easily.

After weighing her options, Orpah took her mother-in-law's advice. She may or may not have been selfish when she made that choice—scripture doesn't tell us. Orpah simply took the logical, time-honored path for a widow and sought remarriage in her own land. Any person of her day would have seen the sense of her decision.

But unknowingly, in aiming for security, Orpah lost out on a lot.

Of course, it wasn't certain Orpah would find a husband when she returned home. Perhaps she did, but scripture never says. Did she ultimately raise a fine family and enjoy marital bliss? It could have happened. But no matter how wonderful her later life may have been, it could not begin to compare to that of Naomi's faithful daughter-in-law, Ruth. Though she was not an Israelite, Ruth ended up marrying a wonderful man—and became one of the forebears of the Messiah. Her faithfulness earned her an unmatched place in Jesus' genealogy.

Sometimes the logical solution to a problem isn't God's solution. He may ask us to risk all by doing what seems illogical. As we begin to walk down that path, doubts may assail us. Let's remember, though, that while stepping out in faith may appear risky, it's only because we're looking at it from a human point of view. Anyone who follows God is surrounded by His powerful hands. What can harm a Christian who places complete trust in her Lord?

Orpah went for worldly security. Ruth sought God's security. While one looked at today's world, the other obeyed God and received a special place in eternity. Who made the better choice?

PENINNAH

Whenever the day came for Elkanah to sacrifice,
he would give portions of the meat to his wife
Peninnah and to all her sons and daughters.
But to Hannah he gave a double portion because he loved her,
and the LORD had closed her womb.

1 SAMUEL 1:4–5

Peninnah was the "other woman" in Elkanah and Hannah's marriage. But instead of meeting secretly with Peninnah, Elkanah had brought her home as a second wife. Not that he really loved her—he probably just wanted her to have the children that Hannah could not seem to bear.

Though Elkanah loved Hannah best, she had to see this other woman every day and know she shared her husband. And Peninnah had to know she'd never be as treasured as Hannah. Though Peninnah had the blessing of Elkanah's children, she didn't really have his love.

Elkanah did right by his second wife, giving her what was required, but he wasn't as generous to her as he was to Hannah. Knowing she'd always be second best, Peninnah responded in one of those odd ways people react when they feel unloved: She tried to irritate her competition at every opportunity.

Of course, that wasn't going to make her beloved by Elkanah, who certainly would have wished for peace. And it clearly didn't make a friend of Hannah. But can we blame her for not wanting to share her husband? How trapped she must have felt in a marriage with no hope. Though Peninnah had the children and spent her life caring for them, she would always feel second best, underrated, and empty.

What woman could feel happy in such a situation? Since His children's happiness is important to God, from the very start He designed marriage as a one-man, one-woman relationship (see Genesis 2:24). The patriarchs who tried to change that plan paid the price for their sin. Scripture never gives an example of a happily married threesome.

This kind of marriage didn't work in Elkanah's day, and it won't work in ours, either. That's why God calls us all to be faithful to one spouse—in both body and spirit. Sometimes that takes a huge quantity of patience. But, as Elkanah found, waiting might just prove the best path. Because, after awhile, God allowed Hannah to have children, too. Imagine the grief this family could have avoided, if the husband had trusted God and waited for children in the Lord's timing!

Let's resist the temptation to redesign marriage. God knows just how we are made and provides for our needs. Finding satisfaction in marriage brings a peace multiple relationships can never provide.

PERSIS

Greet Tryphena and Tryphosa,
those women who work hard in the Lord.
Greet my dear friend Persis, another woman
who has worked very hard in the Lord.

ROMANS 16:12

We don't often think of Paul as having a dear woman friend. Timothy, Silas, and other guys might be close to him, but we barely think of the apostle's relationship with women. Perhaps we even think he didn't much like them.

But when Paul listed the hard workers in the Roman church, he added Persis's name and words of high praise. Though his male disciples made great efforts, where does he give them such an accolade?

We don't know what Persis did to build the Roman church. Did she tirelessly bear witness to her friends? Suffer deeply under persecution? Teach the young people of the congregation? Paul doesn't say. We know nothing of her trials and tribulations. A few words simply tell us of her hard work.

Today, when we work diligently in the Lord, do we do it for attention and affirmation? Or would we be pleased if no one knew what role we play in forwarding God's kingdom?

In eternity we'll meet many believers who built God's church. Are they any less important because no one praised them? God's rewards in heaven will not shortchange anyone—even giving a cup of cold water will receive its reward. Are we content to wait for ours?

PETER'S MOTHER-IN-LAW

Jesus left the synagogue and went to the home of Simon.
Now Simon's mother-in-law was suffering from a high fever,
and they asked Jesus to help her.
So he bent over her and rebuked the fever, and it left her.
She got up at once and began to wait on them.

LUKE 4:38–39

In the days before antibiotics and other highly effective medications, a deadly illness was often foreshadowed by a high fever. So, when his mother-in-law was afflicted with a fever, it's no wonder that Simon, whom Jesus later named Peter, called on the Master.

The disciples had seen Jesus' miracles of healing. But now Simon's trust in the Master led him to invite Jesus into his own home, to heal a family member. Jesus, in command of all illnesses, rebuked the fever, which immediately left this woman who is known only by her relationship to Simon. She must have quickly felt the change, since she got up right away to wait on Jesus and four of His disciples—James and John, and Simon and his brother Andrew (see Mark 1:29). That instantaneous restoration of health impacted many lives through these few verses.

We have seen Jesus do many miracles—if not bodily healings, healed hearts and spirits through His gentle touch. Does this encourage us to serve immediately and faithfully? Peter's mother-in-law had the right idea: Serving Jesus is our praise for all He's done for us.

PHOEBE

I commend to you our sister Phoebe,
a servant of the church in Cenchrea.
I ask you to receive her in the Lord in a way
worthy of the saints and to give her any help
she may need from you, for she has been
a great help to many people, including me.

ROMANS 16:1–2

Since it was not uncommon in Paul's day for a writer to introduce the bearer of a message to the ones receiving it, Phoebe may well have delivered his letter to the Romans. She had traveled to Rome from Cenchrea, a seaport near Corinth, perhaps on some business of her own.

The word *servant* indicates she was a deaconess, and a generous one, too, to judge by Paul's approval of her. She had not taken on the job to further her own position in the church. She was active, aiding those who came within her orbit. Though that may have included the women of the Cenchrean church, even leaders like Paul benefited from her ministry.

Are we like Phoebe, giving generously of our time and energy to the church? Or do we prefer to let others take on the work? God is not looking for those who simply accept Him and sit back in an easy chair. Helping others is a great service to Him, as Paul attests. Will we receive such kudos from Jesus when we meet Him in eternity?

PILATE'S WIFE

While Pilate was sitting on the judge's seat,
his wife sent him this message:
"Don't have anything to do with that innocent man,
for I have suffered a great deal today
in a dream because of him."

MATTHEW 27:19

Though she may not have been a believer, God used Pilate's wife to warn the Roman governor that he was about to make a grave error in trying Jesus. Early in the morning, as Pilate was about to start the trial, her message came to him.

Though Pilate had doubts about Jesus' guilt, he seems to have ignored the message from home. Even his wife's concern that testified to the Messiah's innocence, a sort of last-ditch effort to get through to the governor, was pushed aside by the issues of the moment. Pilate unjustly condemned Jesus to die.

Maybe the governor's wife wasn't surprised that he disregarded her dream, but she had bravely tried to do the right thing. Perhaps that helped her live with the results of the trial.

Can we bravely stand up for the truth, even when no one seems likely to listen? If so, we follow in this woman's footsteps. Though others may ignore us, we will have been a voice for God. Are we willing to speak out?

Now Joseph was well-built and handsome,
and after a while his master's wife took notice
of Joseph and said, "Come to bed with me!". . . .
And though she spoke to Joseph day after day,
he refused to go to bed with her or even be with her.
GENESIS 39:6–7, 10

No shy and retiring woman had Potiphar married. She ordered slaves to do her will, even if that was to join her in bed. She always got what she desired—and now she wanted Joseph.

She was probably one of those women who saw sex as recreation. In a rather boring life, she could fill her hours with men. And, with Joseph in charge and Potiphar caring for nothing but his own food, perhaps her husband was careless of his wife. Feeling unloved, she would take any man she could get. Why not the handsome slave Joseph, who was easily within reach?

But Joseph was different. He preferred to obey God, and perhaps he remembered the time his sister Dinah was raped—and all the horror and the trouble that had caused. As a follower of God, Joseph honored marriage. And, in practical terms, he probably wanted to avoid the trouble he'd find if his master discovered such a dalliance.

Potiphar's wife meant to be the downfall of Joseph. When he refused her, she accused him of rape. But, ultimately and ironically, her actions eventually brought Joseph into the second position in all Egypt. He gained authority only slightly less than Pharaoh's.

Though this slave suffered for his stance, God blessed Joseph in a way no one could have imagined. We have no record that he used that authority against his accuser or her husband. Joseph eventually understood that God had been behind it all.

Nothing more is said of Potiphar's wife. If she continued in this lifestyle, she was undoubtedly unhappy. After this, her husband may have watched her more carefully. Or perhaps he gave up on her entirely.

This unnamed woman warns us that sex is not a game. Joseph could have given in to her demands because, as a slave, he could suffer for disobedience to his mistress. But he stood his ground and, because of it, God gave him great responsibility. Those who can be trusted in their sexual life can be trusted in high office, too.

Would anyone have wanted Potiphar's wife in a position of great authority?

PRISCILLA

Greet Priscilla and Aquila, my fellow workers in Christ Jesus.
They risked their lives for me.
Not only I but all the churches
of the Gentiles are grateful to them.
ROMANS 16:3–4

The Bible never speaks of Priscilla (who is also called Prisca) without mentioning Aquila, and vice versa. They are a matched set, like pepper and salt shakers. But the salt they spread was the Good News.

How did Priscilla and Aquila risk their lives for Paul? We don't know. But we have some details about their stalwart leadership in the early church. Acts 18 tells of their meeting with the apostle and some of the work they did within the church. But it does not speak of a conversion, so this Jewish couple may already have believed when they met the apostle.

Except for one instance, Priscilla's name appears first, causing some scholars to think she might have had more worldly stature than her husband. Whoever the world thought was more important, Priscilla and Aquila took on every mission together.

From Corinth, where they had met Paul, this couple from Asia Minor went to Ephesus with him. First Corinthians 16:19 shows they stayed there and established a church in their home. The apostle left that church in their capable hands.

When Apollos came through the city, preaching something less than the entire gospel, Priscilla and Aquila took him in and taught him about the resurrection and the Holy Spirit's baptism. They must have been successful in their schooling, since the church in Ephesus supported Apollos when he moved on to Achaia, giving him a letter of introduction to the believers there. They never would have sent a false teacher to another church.

In Acts and the epistles, we get only tantalizing glimpses of this couple's lives. But they appear to have been a real marital team, working together to further the gospel. Paul calls them "fellow workers," so doubtless they spread the Good News in their city and anywhere else they traveled. In each place where he mentions them, he speaks highly of Priscilla and Aquila and their work.

If you're married, are you and your husband a spiritual team? If you're not married, do you want to marry someone you can partner with in the faith? Priscilla and Aquila show every believer how wonderful such a collaboration can be. What is stronger than two people joined in Christ, working to further His kingdom? Nothing.

THE PROVERBS 31 WOMAN

A wife of noble character who can find?
She is worth far more than rubies.
Her husband has full confidence in her and lacks nothing of value.
She brings him good, not harm, all the days of her life.
She selects wool and flax and works with eager hands.
She is like the merchant ships, bringing her food from afar.
She gets up while it is still dark; she provides food
for her family and portions for her servant girls. . . .
She sets about her work vigorously;
her arms are strong for her tasks.

PROVERBS 31:10–15, 17

What an intimidating woman this is. She makes today's career woman look absolutely lazy! Yet we haven't even gotten to the end of her description.

Okay, maybe she isn't one real woman. She's a picture of what the faithful believer can do when empowered by God. A good wife might not accomplish all these things in the same day, either. (Let her sleep in occasionally—she's going to need it, with all those tasks ahead.) Maybe she won't even do them all in the same year. But she gives us a lifelong picture of what it means to be a Christian woman.

Read to the end of Proverbs 31, and you'll know where God says to put your efforts. You'll also learn that He has nothing against a woman who runs a business, juggles many tasks, and still loves her family.

Who is this woman? It could be you.

THE QUEEN OF SHEBA

When the queen of Sheba heard about the fame of Solomon
and his relation to the name of the LORD,
she came to test him with hard questions.

1 KINGS 10:1

News of Solomon's wisdom had penetrated a country
in southwest Arabia, known for its trade with India and
great wealth (see Psalm 72:15; Isaiah 60:6). Sheba's queen
probably wanted to confer with Solomon on trade issues,
but perhaps news of his acumen made her visit in person,
rather than sending a representative. Since she brought
many expensive gifts, she obviously wanted to impress
Israel's king.

Even the best Sheba had to offer fell short of Solomon's
court, for the queen was overwhelmed. When she praised
him, the queen touched on the reason for his blessings of
goods and mind: "Because of the LORD's eternal love for
Israel, he has made you king to maintain justice and righ-
teousness" (1 Kings 10:9).

Where does true wisdom come from? Not from education or position or anything else of human origin. This
probably pagan queen got it right: God alone can give a
mind that understands so much.

Though we may never rival Solomon's understanding,
God will give us wisdom, too. Like Sheba's queen, we simply need to seek it.

RACHEL

Leah had weak eyes,
but Rachel was lovely in form, and beautiful.
Jacob was in love with Rachel and said,
"I'll work for you seven years
in return for your younger daughter Rachel."
GENESIS 29:17–18

Jacob did what Mama wanted—he looked for a woman of his own people to marry. At his father's bidding, he traveled to his uncle Laban's home and sought out one of Laban's daughters as his wife.

At a well near Laban's home, Jacob met Rachel the shepherdess and watered her sheep. Surely he wanted to impress this beautiful woman! And he did just that. Rachel went home to her father and told him about his sister's son.

Within a month, Jacob was deeply in love. To secure his bride, he promised to work for Laban for seven years, "but they seemed like only a few days to him because of his love for her" (Genesis 29:20).

At the end of those years, they had a wedding celebration. But that first night Laban duped his nephew by bringing his daughter Leah to the new son-in-law's bed. Jacob didn't discover the deception until morning. Angry at Laban, he still demanded the woman he loved.

Rachel's father promised her to Jacob as a second wife, setting up a terrible situation for all involved. Rachel undoubtedly felt used by her father's duplicity and betrayed by her sister. After all, for seven years everyone had known of Jacob's love for her. And then there was the embarrassment of it all. Those emotions would overwhelm Rachel her whole life.

But Jacob still loved Rachel best. As they started their married life, she must have felt the promise of their love, only to have it denied as babies failed to appear. Jacob and Rachel's great passion did not bear the fruit that seemed so necessary to a woman's happiness.

Instead, Leah had the children. And the more children she had, the more Leah hoped her husband would love her. But, after four sons, nothing had changed in her emotional life. Jacob still loved Rachel, and Leah, too, felt betrayed.

Following in Sarai's footsteps, the loved but angry and jealous Rachel gave her maid, Bilhah, to Jacob to have children in her place. Rachel named Bilhah's second son *Naphtali*, meaning "my struggle." Rachel proclaimed, "I have had a great struggle with my sister, and I have won" (Genesis 30:8). Obviously family harmony didn't live in these tents.

Leah, seeing that Bilhah was having children, did the same as Rachel, giving her maid, Zilpah, to Jacob. So two more children were born into this unhappy family. Then Leah had three more children, including Jacob's only daughter. Finally God remembered Rachel, and she bore Joseph, who would one day be second only to Pharaoh.

Jacob wanted to return to his homeland. For a while, Laban convinced him to stay by offering Jacob whatever he wanted. Once Jacob had developed a large flock, though, he fled, with the goodwill of his wives. There was nothing to bind them to their home. Laban followed, searching for the household gods Rachel had hidden in her tent. He didn't find them, as Rachel was sitting on them, saying she couldn't stand during her monthly "custom of women" (Genesis 31:35 KJV). After Laban, the deceiving father, had himself been deceived, Jacob and his family went on their way.

Jacob settled in Bethel, where Rachel had a second son. But shortly after his birth, she died. Though she asked that he be named *Ben-Oni*, "son of my trouble," Jacob called him the more positive *Benjamin*, "son of my right hand."

Rachel and her sister mothered the sons who began Israel's twelve tribes. Though the lives of Rachel and Leah were much less than smooth, God kept His promise to make a large nation of Israel.

Like these two women, we may experience hardship due to others' decisions. But God is always in control, planning things we have yet to see. If Rachel had known she'd have two sons, would she have started the baby competition with her sister? Maybe if she'd waited, she would have had four more sons, to make up those twelve tribes. We'll never know.

But we do know we can always trust our Lord. No one derails His plans.

RAHAB

Then Joshua son of Nun secretly sent two spies from Shittim.
"Go, look over the land," he said, "especially Jericho."
So they went and entered the house of a prostitute
named Rahab and stayed there.

JOSHUA 2:1

Innkeeper or prostitute? Scholars have pondered which
Rahab was, since the word used here for "prostitute" could
be translated either way. It's probable this woman of Jericho
both ran an inn and offered the guests a second service on
the side.

Whatever her sexual morality, Rahab had no trouble
lying about Joshua's men when Jericho's king asked her to
bring out the two Israelite spies he'd heard of. Well prepared, Rahab had already hidden the Israelites on her roof,
under drying stalks of flax. Instead of directing the king's
officers upstairs, she told them the men had left the city
before the gates had closed for the night. So the king's
men set off on a wild goose chase.

Had Rahab already heard such wonderful things about
the Lord that she began to realize how empty a life of
prostitution had become? Since she knew quite a lot about
Joshua and his people—and was willing to put her life on
the line for them—she must have come to belief before the
two men knocked on her door.

Rahab was brave, willing to help these spies, and faithful in carrying out their directions. Though she must have

feared the damage Joshua and his people could cause, she threw in her lot with the strange men. All she asked was that her family be spared. The men agreed quickly, so using a rope, she lowered them out of her window. Perhaps the spies had chosen her house with this in mind, for it sat upon the city wall, a convenient place for two men who wanted to leave surreptitiously. They quickly obeyed Rahab's directions to "head for the hills."

Before they left, the spies made Rahab promise not to tell anyone where they were heading. In return, they would be faithful to their promise and save her family. But she would have to gather her entire family together and hang a scarlet cord out the window she'd use for their escape.

Once the king's men stopped looking for them, the two spies returned to Joshua and told him what Rahab had reported: The people were terrified of the Israelites' coming. She was right, for as soon as the Israelites crossed the Jordan, the Canaanites lost their nerve. Jericho shut its gates, and no one went in or out.

Once "the walls came tumbling down" by God's power, Joshua sent the two spies to make good on their promise and save Rahab and her family. After their rescue, they were placed in an encampment outside Israel's camp. Since the newcomers had been involved in a pagan religion, Israel needed to be sure they'd turned away from their past before allowing them into the camp.

Rahab became one of the few women mentioned in Jesus' lineage (see Matthew 1:5). She may not have had a perfect background, but she was a changed woman. When this former prostitute showed her faith, it was so all could see. Hebrews 11, the faith chapter, lists her among many of the Bible's great saints (see verse 31). James 2:25 tells us that Rahab was justified by her actions.

Faith is not only a matter of mental assent or a powerful spiritual experience. Our actions show where our hearts are. And Rahab's heart was surely with God.

Do we show our faith as clearly as this former prostitute? Will our actions show whose side we are on in the battle between Christianity and unbelief? Like Rahab, we need to be brave, willing, and faithful in doing His will. We never know when God may send someone to our door!

REBEKAH

Isaac brought her into the tent of his mother Sarah,
and he married Rebekah.
So she became his wife, and he loved her;
and Isaac was comforted after his mother's death.
GENESIS 24:67

How wonderful is the romance between Isaac and Rebekah.
He loved her so much that she was his only wife. In an
age of polygamy, their love must have stood out from their
neighbors'.

Even before they met, God worked to bring their love
into being. Abraham sent his chief servant on a trip. This
caring father feared the influence of the pagan Canaanites
and wanted the best in marriage for his son. So a servant
traveled to Abraham's own homeland to find a wife for
Isaac.

Trudging across the desert with camels bearing gifts, the
man approached the town of Nahor. There he found the
beautiful and generous Rebekah who both gave him a drink
and offered to water the camels. When he discovered her
father was Abraham's brother, the faithful servant worshiped
God. *This* was the right woman!

Rebekah invited the man to the house of her father,
Bethuel. There it was quickly decided Rebekah should be
Isaac's wife. Along with her nurse, Rebekah traveled to meet
her new husband.

Even if Isaac didn't experience love at first sight, it

didn't take long for him to fall for this beautiful woman. He brought her to his mother's tent, married her, and loved her. As was the case for so many Bible women, there would be no quick conception and birthing. But after Isaac prayed, God finally gave Rebekah not one child, but twins.

The phrase "easy pregnancy" was not part of Rebekah's vocabulary for those nine months. The children struggled within her, and God told her she had two nations in her womb. One would be stronger than the other, and the older would serve the younger.

Rebekah delivered two sons. The first was red and hairy, so he was called *Esau*, which means "hairy." The second child grasped this brother's heel, so they named him *Jacob,* or "grasps the heel." Esau became a hunter, while Jacob turned into a homebody. Though Isaac loved his first son, Rebekah loved Jacob best. One day, the hungry Esau sold his birthright as eldest son to Isaac for a red lentil stew.

When famine touched their country, Isaac moved to the land of the Philistines. Because Rebekah was so beautiful, he feared the men of that land would kill him to get her—so Isaac caller her his sister. When King Abimelech discovered the deception, he issued a stern reprimand—and then protected Isaac. Later, King Abimelech said to Isaac, "Move away from us; you have become too powerful for us" (Genesis 26:16).

So Isaac left, eventually settling in Beersheba. Esau, meanwhile, married two Hittite women, bringing sorrow to the family.

When Isaac became old and blind, he wanted to bless

Esau as his firstborn, but Rebekah conspired with Jacob to gain that blessing for the younger son instead. Ignoring God's promise that her favorite son would have the place of importance, she helped Jacob deceive her blind husband. Rebekah prepared a goat dinner, and Jacob brought it to his father, pretending to be Esau. Jacob received the blessing, but at a great price. He had to flee Esau's anger and never saw his mother again.

We don't know what Rebekah was thinking when she cooked up this plot. Did her trust in God fail? Maybe—or maybe she thought she was helping God's will along. Either way, it certainly wasn't her most successful meal.

A woman of faith is not judged on a one-time act, but her whole life record. Rebekah, beautiful and generous in her youth, becomes a conniving woman who will do anything to see her favorite son benefit.

God calls us to be consistently faithful, to run the whole race well. When we are young, with the world before us, we may think we can do nothing wrong. But it takes character and deep faith to build a consistent testimony for a lifetime. The hard times and doubts come, but those who remember God's promises and cling to them never fail.

God walks beside us, just as He walked with Rebekah. If she had sought His will before cooking a goat dinner, things could have been so very different.

RHODA

Peter knocked at the outer entrance,
and a servant girl named Rhoda came to answer the door.
When she recognized Peter's voice, she was so overjoyed
she ran back without opening it and exclaimed,
"Peter is at the door!"
ACTS 12:13–14

What joy lit up Rhoda's face when she saw the apostle Peter standing on her mistress's doorstep. Peter, who only minutes before had been locked in a Roman jail! Delighted at his release, Rhoda darted off to tell Mary, John Mark's mother. But she had forgotten to open the door, so Peter patiently kept knocking.

When Rhoda reported the news to the Christians gathered in Mary's home, she didn't get the expected response. "You're crazy!" they essentially replied. When she wouldn't give up, they decided it must be his angel. Only when they saw for themselves would they believe this simple servant's testimony. Peter came inside and told the story of his miraculous release by an angel, urged them to tell others of his release, and then departed.

Though many of higher rank doubted her testimony, lowly Rhoda stood firm. Even getting them to check it out for themselves was difficult, but her persistence succeeded. Do we need the same persistence in our own faith? Doubters may come to belief, if only we stand firm.

RUTH

*But Ruth replied, "Don't urge me to leave you
or to turn back from you.
Where you go I will go, and where you stay I will stay.
Your people will be my people and your God my God."*
RUTH 1:16

She wasn't Jewish but belonged to a pagan people. She had
nothing in this world to gain and everything to lose—yet
Ruth clung to her mother-in-law and refused to return to
her homeland when Naomi left for her own land of Israel.

Ruth, her sister-in-law Orpah, and Naomi had seen
their husbands die. Now, with no one to care for them and
no career with which to earn a living, things looked very
bleak. Yet when Orpah left, Ruth remained steadfast. If she
was going to face hard times, it would not be alone.

Perhaps Ruth's husband and his family had been such
excellent witnesses to their faith that Ruth didn't want
to miss this God they worshiped. From her actions in
the book that bears her name, it's likely she was already a
believer. Or maybe she simply loved Naomi enough not
to walk away. But Ruth was a woman of character who
followed her mother-in-law into dire circumstances—and
saved them both from utter destitution.

Together, the women traveled to Bethlehem, where
Naomi declared her affliction to her one-time neighbors.
But the life that looked so dire was not to end in tragedy,
for her faithful relatives would come to her aid.

First among them was Ruth, who quickly went to work picking up the leftovers from the barley harvest. God commanded landowners to leave some grain for the poor, and Ruth was not too humble to join others in gathering what she could to support herself and Naomi. As God (not luck) would have it, she ended up gathering the grain in the fields of Boaz, who was related to Naomi's husband, Elimelech.

The industrious woman stood out to Boaz, and he commanded his servants to watch over her, making certain she had enough grain. He told Ruth to stay close to his servant girls for protection. He even told her to share his workers' food and water.

Humbled, Ruth wondered why he would be so generous. Boaz replied that he had heard what she had done for Naomi. But this wealthy landowner, who was a close enough relative to be a kinsman-redeemer, was about to do even more for the women.

A kinsman-redeemer was responsible for protecting family members in need. In Naomi's case, her nearest relative could not act. So Naomi told Ruth to go to the threshing floor and lie at Boaz's feet, a way of asking him to marry her. Touched by Ruth's willingness to marry an older man, and reminded that he was a close enough relative to be the kinsman-redeemer, Boaz took on that role. He took care of the legalities and announced that he would marry Ruth. Having received the elders' blessing on his proposal to a Moabite who had been so faithful to Naomi, he followed through on his promise.

Boaz and Ruth's son, Obed, would care for Naomi in her old age—but more than that, he would become the grandfather of King David. Even greater, he became part of the lineage of the Messiah.

Ruth's is the story of an unbelieving woman who came to faith, a poor woman who was richly blessed, a woman who was redeemed by one who pictures what the Savior does for all who come to Him in faith. Ruth was liberated from physical and spiritual need.

The Lord who rescued Ruth still rescues us today. Are we in need physically, spiritually, or emotionally? God will bless us, if only we have the character to cling to Him. Do we have doubts about our future? He has not forgotten us. Though we may gather grain for a while, He will not leave us empty. For Jesus, our kinsman-redeemer, married us when we came to Him. He will never leave us or forsake us.

SALOME, JAMES AND
JOHN'S MOTHER

*Then the mother of Zebedee's sons
came to Jesus with her sons and,
kneeling down, asked a favor of him.
"What is it you want?" he asked.
She said, "Grant that one of these two sons
of mine may sit at your right and the other
at your left in your kingdom."*

MATTHEW 20:20–21

By combining Mark 15:40 and Matthew 27:56, we know
the name of Zebedee's wife. Her husband and sons, James
and John, worked what must have been a fairly extensive
family fishing business, since Zebedee had hired men working for him (see Mark 1:20) and Simon was in a partner-
ship with them, too (see Luke 5:10).

Salome had a fairly comfortable life. And with two fine
sons, what more did she need?

When James and John suddenly left their nets and followed Jesus, it must have been a surprise to Salome and her
husband. But it probably wasn't a bone of contention in
the family. She may have been proud of her sons' standing
with the Master.

Obviously Salome wanted her wonderful sons to "get
ahead" not only on earth, but in eternity. That's why she
asked for key places for them in His kingdom. But Jesus
couldn't promise that. She must have been humbled by

His denial, but it did not damage her faith—she's one of the women at both Christ's crucifixion and resurrection (see Mark 15:40; 16:1).

Salome had a good life with some unexpected bends in the road. She could have become angry when her sons left the family business, but obviously she supported them. Nor did anger ruin her faith when Jesus redirected her desires away from greatness for her children.

Like Salome, we need to accept the changes God makes in our lives and obey His will. Then we may find great joy in the life God designs for us—His plan may be marvelous beyond our expectations.

SALOME THE DANCER

*On Herod's birthday the daughter
of Herodias danced for them
and pleased Herod so much that he promised
with an oath to give her whatever she asked.*

MATTHEW 14:6–7

Josephus, not scripture, records her name, but the Bible tells of her heinous act. At the request of her mother, Salome asked for the death of John the Baptist; Mama Herodias had an ax to grind with John, who had publicly condemned her marriage to Herod.

On her stepfather's birthday, Salome performed an erotic dance before him and his guests. Pleased, Herod offered her whatever she wanted. Who knows what young Salome might have asked for herself—it was her mother's idea to request John the Baptist's head on a platter. The king didn't like the idea, but since he'd promised and she'd requested in public, he felt he had to make good. So John literally lost his head.

Though her request may have pleased her mother, this gruesome gift was not otherwise of much use to Salome. And certainly the guests did not appreciate having their dinner so discomposed.

From Salome we learn to ask wisely for the things we want. What we desire may change someone else's life—hers ended John's existence. Salome would hardly be remembered, if she hadn't done this evil thing. Do we want to be remembered for our worst request?

Manoah. . .had a wife who was sterile and remained childless.
The angel of the LORD appeared to her and said,
"You are sterile and childless,
but you are going to conceive and have a son.
Now see to it that you drink no wine or other fermented drink
and that you do not eat anything unclean,
because you will conceive and give birth to a son.
No razor may be used on his head,
because the boy is to be a Nazirite, set apart to God from birth,
and he will begin the deliverance of Israel
from the hands of the Philistines."

JUDGES 13:2–5

This unnamed woman is not the only one in scripture who waited long to have a child and then had an important son. Samson's mother, though, received the extra command not to drink anything fermented or eat anything unclean. For Samson was to be a Nazirite.

He would take a special vow of dedication to God (see Numbers 6:1–21), which the angel outlined to his mother. Though many people made a Nazirite vow that lasted only awhile, Samson was dedicated to God from the time of his conception, because this boy would begin the deliverance of Israel from the Philistines.

Samson's mother understood the favor God had shown in sending the angel to her and then to her husband. Dedicated to God, this couple must have raised Samson with God's promise constantly in mind, if Manoah's concern for the child's upbringing is any indication (see Judges 13:8–14).

As he grew, God blessed Samson, and one day, His Spirit stirred the young man, empowering him for his mission. If only Samson had continued as he began. For though he became Israel's judge, he did not remain separated to God— at least not in his romantic life. He married a Philistine, against his parents' desire, and when his marriage failed, he became entangled with Delilah, who led him into sin and ultimately to his death.

Though his mother must have grieved over Samson's moral failures, God was still faithful. Even in these unlikely situations, Samson began the deliverance of Israel. Though enslaved to the Philistines, Samson destroyed his enemies' temple and killed many of them, too.

Do you know a Christian mother who has painfully watched children turn from the Lord of their childhood, making her wonder what she might have done wrong along the way? In our sin-filled world, no parent is perfect—and neither is any child. But God can work all things to good, despite the sorrow of wrong choices on both sides. His plan can never be destroyed, even by an unruly child or a less-than-perfect mother.

Now a man named Ananias,
together with his wife Sapphira,
also sold a piece of property.
With his wife's full knowledge
he kept back part of the money for himself,
but brought the rest and put it at the apostles' feet.

ACTS 5:1–2

You can't fool God. But Ananias and Sapphira had to learn that lesson the hard way. The *really* hard way.

In a time when the church was persecuted, many believers, like Barnabas (see Acts 4:36–37), gave generously, from the heart. But Ananias and Sapphira's greedy hearts combined their desire for money with a wish to be well thought of in the church. Since they balked at losing all their investment, together they hatched a shortcut plot to sell some property and give money to the church—just not *all* the money.

When Ananias told the church of his gift, Peter, prompted by the Holy Spirit, confronted the deceiver with his lie. It wasn't that Peter objected to his not giving all the money to the congregation—what angered Peter was Ananias's lie that he *had* given all the money, when he had actually kept back a portion. This lie, the apostle pointed out, was not aimed toward men but at God.

As Peter's words hit his ears, the deceitful man died. The young men of the church came forward and immediately took care of Ananias's burial.

Three hours later, the unwitting Sapphira came in. Peter asked the price she and her husband had gotten for the land. From her mouth popped the fraud she and Ananias had agreed on. Peter demanded, "How could you agree to test the Spirit of the Lord? Look! The feet of the men who buried your husband are at the door, and they will carry you out also" (Acts 5:9).

Sapphira also died on the spot, and the congregation buried her next to her husband. As a result of this couple's example, the whole church feared doing wrong.

We don't want to follow in Sapphira's footsteps, but in the path of the Christians who learned from her lesson. Sapphira wanted to *look* good, but not *be* good. Like that early church we need to fear and avoid wrongdoing. Because even if we lie and don't expire immediately, a little part of us does die—our spirits diminish a bit every time we do wrong.

Sure, we can receive forgiveness, but how much better never to sin. Then we become good witnesses to our Savior, and new life—not death—begins.

SARAH

"I will bless her and will surely give you a son by her.
I will bless her so that she will be the mother of nations;
kings of peoples will come from her."

GENESIS 17:16

God promised to raise up a great nation from a couple who had yet to have any children and pledged to give them the whole land of Canaan as an everlasting possession. As crazy as that may have sounded, the husband, Abram, and his wife, Sarai, believed God and, with their retinue, set out for Canaan, God's promised land.

After they'd been there awhile, famine came—and Abram and Sarai moved to Egypt. Fearing the Egyptians would kill him to gain his beautiful wife, Abram asked Sarai to allow him to call her his sister. It was partially true—she was his father's daughter by another mother—but Abram failed to mention that she was also his wife.

After noticing Sarai's stunning beauty, Pharaoh took her into his palace. In response, God afflicted the Egyptian ruler and his household with diseases. When Pharaoh discovered the reason, he took Abram to task and tossed him and his wife out of Egypt.

Abram returned to Canaan, where God again promised him land, to be inherited by many offspring. But Sarai, who was at least sixty-five, had yet to have a single child.

As time went on, Abram began to wonder, "So where is this child, Lord?" Would a servant become his heir? Again

God promised a child and made a covenant with Abram.

It's not hard to imagine the doubts that filled the couple's thoughts. Time was wasting. Their best years for reproduction had passed, and no child was in sight. So Sarai decided to generate a child by her slave, Hagar. The babe would be considered Sarai's, and maybe God's promise would be fulfilled. Too bad she didn't check with God before making that choice, for she was bringing great anguish to their family life.

Once Hagar was pregnant, it must have struck Sarai that she herself was at fault for her and Abram's inability to have children. Abram's reproductive parts were clearly working. When Hagar conceived, she despised her mistress. In return, Sarai treated the servant so badly that Hagar fled. Only God's intervention returned her to the camp.

After the birth of Ishmael, Hagar's son, God confirmed his covenant with Abram and renamed him *Abraham*. Sarai would be called *Sarah*. Again God promised that Sarah would have a son, and his would be the covenant line. A year before the birth, three mysterious men appeared and promised Abraham that Sarah would have a son. Sarah, listening in her tent, laughed at the idea.

Before his son Isaac was born, Abraham proved he hadn't learned one lesson. He returned to the Negev and again claimed Sarah was only his sister. And again, a king—this time of Gerar—took her. But God protected His people, coming in a dream to warn Abimelech of his unintentional wrongdoing. So Sarah was again returned to her husband, along with many gifts, to cover the offense.

Finally, in their old age, Sarah and Abraham had Isaac. But now Hagar and her son became jealous, so Sarah demanded that they leave. God told Abraham to follow his wife's desire. The line He'd promised was from Isaac, not Ishmael, though he, too, would become a great nation.

Then came a great test of faith. God commanded Abraham to sacrifice this son of promise. Scripture doesn't mention Sarah when it tells of this event. Perhaps she didn't find out until after the fact, when her son was saved. But we can easily imagine her emotions in the situation: Fear, doubt, and questioning were replaced by the certainty of God's salvation.

Sarah lived to be 127 years old. When she died, Abraham asked the Hittites for a tomb for her, and they offered him the best available. He bought a choice spot near Mamre for his much-loved wife.

She was not perfect, but her God was. Even after Sarah made a tragic error of judgment and tried to have a son in the wrong way, God confirmed His promises. And she is commended by Him in 1 Peter 3:6, so we can assume she was a woman of real faith, who, under real stress, had a moral failure.

Like Sarah, we do not have to be perfect for God to love us. He has chosen to do that, and He will not change.

SHIPHRAH

The king of Egypt said to the Hebrew midwives,
whose names were Shiphrah and Puah,
"When you help the Hebrew women in childbirth
and observe them on the delivery stool,
if it is a boy, kill him; but if it is a girl, let her live."
EXODUS 1:15–16

Two midwives seem unlikely folks to engage in civil disobedience, but that's just what brave Shiphrah and her coworker Puah did when Pharaoh demanded they kill the Hebrew boys. Because they feared God more than Egypt's ruler, they let the children live—and told the ruler that the women gave birth before they got to them. Did the two women feel guilt over their lie and confess it to God? He did bless them for their stand, despite this wrongdoing.

Since two women could never have helped birth all the Hebrew children, these two were probably in charge of all the Hebrew midwives. They had an important responsibility, but even more, they understood their responsibility to God. When they had to disobey someone, they looked to the good of their souls before their high positions. So God rewarded "them [with] families of their own" (Exodus 1:21).

Are there some things in our own lives that are worth standing up for, no matter what the cost? Losing a job or an important community position might be better than offending God. Will we stand with Shiphrah or Pharaoh?

One day Elisha went to Shunem.
And a well-to-do woman was there,
who urged him to stay for a meal.
So whenever he came by, he stopped there to eat.
2 KINGS 4:8

Her hospitality might seem a small thing, but because she gave generously to the prophet, the Shunammite woman saw amazing things happen in her life.

Her ministry began when she gave Elisha a meal. Soon he stopped by whenever he traveled her way. So the woman decided to provide a room for the prophet to stay in.

This hospitality obviously meant a lot to Elisha, who wanted to give her something in return. When he asked her, this humble but prosperous woman admitted to no need. But the prophet's servant, Gehazi, pointed out that she had no child. So the prophet promised that in a year, God would give her a son.

Perhaps she had given up hope of having a child by her older husband, or maybe there had been miscarriages. But she objected, "No, my lord. . . . Don't mislead your servant, O man of God!" (2 Kings 4:16). Perhaps previous disappointments filled her heart with doubt. But in a year, as the prophet promised, she held a boy in her arms.

One day, when the boy went to join his father and the reapers, his head began to hurt. The servants returned the boy to his mother, who held him on her lap until he died.

This faithful woman, without even telling her husband of their child's death, asked him for a donkey and traveled to see Elisha. Elisha immediately sent Gehazi before him, but nothing the servant did raised the boy. So Elisha came, prayed, and stretched himself on the boy, who immediately revived.

Sometime later, the prophet warned the woman to move, to avoid a famine in her land. So she and her family left for Philistia. When they returned, the husband was no longer living, so the Shunammite went to the king to beg for her house and land back. As she came to him, Gehazi had just finished telling the king of her story. She immediately received everything back, even the income her land had produced during the seven years she'd been gone.

God blesses his faithful servants, even when their service may seem small. Like the Shunammite, we may provide some minor but essential service that has helped move the gospel into others' hearts. Will God forget our faithfulness and fail to repay? Never! Look at the great blessings the Shunammite had for her hospitality.

SYNTYCHE

*I plead with Euodia and I plead with Syntyche
to agree with each other in the Lord.
Yes, and I ask you, loyal yokefellow,
help these women who have contended
at my side in the cause of the gospel,
along with Clement and the rest of my fellow workers,
whose names are in the book of life.*

PHILIPPIANS 4:2–3

Maybe Syntyche got into an argument with Euodia about how they should help the poor of Philippi, or perhaps she thought the church kitchen should be painted a different color. It didn't have to be a large issue that started their disagreement, but it clearly affected the whole congregation.

Faithful Christians don't always agree. Sometimes their personal preferences don't align perfectly, and that can cause stress and contention. It doesn't mean that either has given up the faith. But all believers need to "agree to disagree in love," as John Wesley said. Their personal preferences should not cause damage to the gospel.

When you have a difference of opinion with another believer in your congregation, do you deal with it in love, or does it become an opportunity to battle each other? You don't have to love everything your brother or sister does—just agree with that person that in Christ you will work together for His kingdom, not your own aims.

THE SYROPHOENICIAN WOMAN

In fact, as soon as she heard about him,
a woman whose little daughter was possessed
by an evil spirit came and fell at his feet.
The woman was a Greek, born in Syrian Phoenicia.
She begged Jesus to drive the demon out of her daughter.

MARK 7:25–26

Though Jesus was trying to get away from the crowds, one desperate Gentile woman followed Him, fell at His feet, and begged for help. Disappointingly, Jesus replied, "I was sent only to the lost sheep of Israel" (Matthew 15:24). Yet still she persisted in asking for His help for her much-loved child.

But Jesus objected, saying, "It is not right to take the children's bread and toss it to their dogs" (Mark 7:27).

She could have become angry at being compared to a dog, for dogs were not favored in Jewish society. Instead, this humble woman agreed, but pointed out that she wasn't asking much—even dogs eat the crumbs from the master's table. Not only did this mother's faith and determination win the daughter's healing, she became a preview of the message of salvation Paul would carry to the Gentiles.

When we face faith challenges, do we stand as firm as this unnamed woman? Though success seems doubtful, do we trust in God rather than our own abilities? If so, in the end, we will enjoy God's blessing, too.

TAMAR, JUDAH'S DAUGHTER-IN-LAW

Judah then said to his daughter-in-law Tamar,
"Live as a widow in your father's house
until my son Shelah grows up."
For he thought,
"He may die too, just like his brothers."
So Tamar went to live in her father's house.

GENESIS 38:11

Tamar's father-in-law, Judah, thought she was a curse against his sons. She had married his two oldest sons, successively, for the custom of the day was for a second son to give his older brother's widow a child as heir. Both of Judah's sons were wicked, though, so God saw to it that they died. Tamar, however, got the blame.

When it came to marrying his third son to Tamar, Judah balked. Instead he sent her back to her family and only *promised* Shelah to her. Time went by, and the marriage never took place. So Tamar hatched a plan.

Pretending to be a prostitute, Tamar wooed the unsuspecting Judah. Since her face was covered, he never recognized her as his daughter-in-law. As a pledge of payment for services that were about to be rendered, Tamar requested Judah leave his seal, its cord, and his staff in her possession. Judah gave them to her and slept with her.

Their liaison resulted in pregnancy. Three months later, still completely unaware of his own role in the situation,

Judah was told that his daughter-in-law was with child. He demanded Tamar be burned to death for prostitution. That's when she showed him the belongings he had left with the "prostitute."

Once he knew he was the father, Judah admitted he had wronged Tamar and that her cause was righteous. Out of this union, God gave Tamar twin boys.

God had compassion on Tamar and gave her the children who would provide for her, since her father-in-law had not done so. Though her methods were wrong, her cause was not—and God gave her aid.

We, too, can count on God's help when we seek it righteously. But, unlike Tamar, let's not forget to obey His laws, too.

TAMAR, DAVID'S DAUGHTER

In the course of time,
Amnon son of David fell in love with Tamar,
the beautiful sister of Absalom son of David.
Amnon became frustrated to the point of illness
on account of his sister Tamar,
for she was a virgin, and it seemed impossible
for him to do anything to her.

2 SAMUEL 13:1–2

What Amnon called love was pure lust. It took only the whisper of a false counselor for the young man to begin a plot that led to his destruction.

At that counselor's advice, he pretended to be sick. Then Amnon asked his father to have Tamar come to his place and prepare food for him. So she came and baked bread—though bread wasn't what Tamar's half brother was really interested in. He got her alone and asked her to sleep with him.

Horrified, the virtuous Tamar tried to warn him of his desire's danger. But when he couldn't persuade her, Amnon raped her. Immediately his guilt turned to anger, and he tossed her out of his house. Distraught, Tamar put ashes on her head and tore her robes, indicating what had happened to her. Then she headed for her brother Absalom's house, where she found comfort and support.

Since King David did nothing about the wrong done to his daughter, in time her brother Absalom took matters into his own hands. Two years after the event, he plotted Amnon's death. Not long after, he conspired to gain the throne.

Have you ever been in Tamar's situation, innocently walking into trouble, which exploded in your face, bringing great damage with it? As Christians, we must live innocently, but not expect wicked people to do the same. Guarding ourselves against sin, we also need to guard against sinners.

TRYPHENA

Greet Tryphena and Tryphosa,
those women who work hard in the Lord.
ROMANS 16:12

There are plenty of Tryphenas and Tryphosas in the church today—women who work hard to spread the gospel, care for the hurting, and help others grow in Christ. Paul didn't denigrate or ignore the women who supported his ministry across the map. He knew he could not work effectively without them and remembered some of them in the greetings of his epistles. Who knows what great things came from their daily ministries—work that may have seemed unimportant at the time.

Is there a Tryphena in your church? Help and encourage her. Learn from her willingness to serve and spend time with her, so you can absorb some of the things that have made her a successful Christian.

Scripture gives us little more than Tryphena's name and the apostle's commendation. But with this verse we see how important our service to God is, even to the most important leader. This "unimportant" woman received a reward on earth and even greater ones in heaven, just like today's faithful women will be approved by Jesus in eternity.

VASHTI

On the seventh day, when King Xerxes
was in high spirits from wine,
he commanded the seven eunuchs who served him. . .
to bring before him Queen Vashti, wearing her royal crown,
in order to display her beauty to the people and nobles,
for she was lovely to look at.
But when the attendants delivered the king's command,
Queen Vashti refused to come.
Then the king became furious and burned with anger.
ESTHER 1:10–12

Any modest woman can understand why Queen Vashti preferred not to appear before the king and his courtiers—they'd just enjoyed a seven-day drinking party. But refusing the king's wish was a dangerous act, for it made Xerxes look as if he had no control over his own wife, let alone his country. Instead of showing off his lovely queen, the king was made to feel small. And kings of large empires don't like feeling small—especially when their wives generate the feeling.

Xerxes' counselors were immediately called. After a quick huddle, they gave their paranoid opinion: All the women in the kingdom, following the example of the queen, would soon refuse to obey their husbands. This had to be stopped immediately! Vashti should be stripped of her rank and never again be allowed to see the king.

Maybe this opinion reflected their own relationships with their wives more than the truth. Or maybe, as guests of the party, they'd been whooping it up a bit too much and were at less than their wisest. But the king took their advice, and Vashti was no longer queen.

The Bible doesn't tell us exactly why Vashti took this dangerous step. Perhaps she didn't want to be shown off at the party, or maybe she had another reason for not appearing. Whatever the cause, this action pushed her off her throne and out of the history books, at least for a while.

Because of Vashti's stand, Esther became queen—and the beautiful young Jewess was in a position to save her people when Haman wanted to kill them. God used Vashti's disobedience to protect His own people, who were enslaved by this powerful ruler.

Ironically, Vashti didn't entirely drop out of history. When her son Artaxerxes became king, she again held power as queen mother.

God's power worked even in the life of this pagan queen. She lost her throne, and Esther saved her people. But in the end, justice came to Vashti, too.

God is in control of all our lives, even when that seems unlikely. When we face hopeless situations, when we seem to be punished for our faith, and when we suffer for no apparent reason, God has not deserted us. We may not see His purpose or justice until the end, but we can be certain He will prevail—just as he did for both Esther and Vashti.

THE WIDOW OF ZAREPHATH

Then the word of the LORD came to [Elijah]:
"Go at once to Zarephath of Sidon and stay there.
I have commanded a widow in that place
to supply you with food."
1 KINGS 17:8–9

When the prophet Elijah prophesied a famine over Israel, he didn't mean the food shortage would affect only the wicked King Ahab. Even the prophet didn't have much to eat, so God fed him by sending ravens with food. (Though it was effective, it doesn't seem like the most appetizing method of delivery.)

But once the prophet's water source dried up, God directed Elijah to Zarephath, a Gentile city. It was home to Israel's enemies and a poor woman who was making a last meal for herself and her son.

The widow didn't have a secret store of food and water, just a great need. And at first she must have doubted the wisdom of sharing what little she had. But her small sacrifice gave great benefit. Amazingly, her only sustenance—an almost empty jar of flour and a bit of oil with which to bake—would not disappear until God sent the rains again.

Awhile later, the woman's son became ill and died. Emotionally wounded, this mother reacted against the man she saw as causing the problem. The woman said to Elijah, "What do you have against me, man of God? Did you come to remind me of my sin and kill my son?" (1 Kings 17:18).

Elijah took the boy, laid him on his bed, and passionately cried out to God to restore his life. God responded, and the boy lived. The mother responded with belief in Elijah as a man of God and in the truth of his message.

God could have continued Elijah's previous arrangements, with the prophet camped out in a gorge, being fed by ravens. God could even have provided a new source of water when the first one dried up. Instead, He sent His prophet to a poor woman of an enemy nation, one who seemed unlikely to be able to help. Of course, the aid she provided was really from God, not her—but God graciously allowed this woman of no stature to become part of His plan of salvation.

God reached out to a woman who had nothing to offer and used her to accomplish much. He loves the weak ones and wants to draw them to Himself. The strong and powerful may easily resist His Word, but the weak and those of no stature seek that one last meal that brings salvation. Let us not despise these spiritually poor people.

As he looked up, Jesus saw the rich
putting their gifts into the temple treasury.
He also saw a poor widow put in two very small copper coins.
"I tell you the truth," he said, "this poor widow
has put in more than all the others.
All these people gave their gifts out of their wealth;
but she out of her poverty put in all she had to live on."

LUKE 21:1–4

In just a few words, we get a picture of two kinds of people: the wealthy and perhaps somewhat generous givers who could put bags of money in the temple vaults, and a woman who gave much more.

Jesus had just warned his disciples of the love the religious leaders had for places of honor and the gain they made from defenseless widows. At that moment, a generous woman walked into the treasury and dropped in her tiny offering. How could her almost valueless coins compare to the greater gifts? While the rich gave of their extra money, she had deposited all her income into the "Bank of God."

What a sacrifice that must have been. Can you imagine her thinking beforehand: *I need to give something, but this is all I have. How will I have enough food? What if I have a crisis?* Whatever her worries might have been, the woman put her complete trust in God and dropped the coins into the temple chest. Maybe she gave the two mites, instead of one, because the single mite would not even have bought her a loaf of bread.

Can we have any doubt that God blessed her richly for this incredibly generous giving?

This humble woman gives us a painful example. If we look at ourselves honestly, we probably have to admit that we're more like the rich men bringing their offerings than the woman who "put in all she had to live on." We may plan our giving, working it into our budgets, but she gave her whole budget. She gave 100 percent, while many faithful Christians today squawk at giving a small portion of their income.

We cannot give too much to God. He's not demanding destitution for us, but calling us to give our all—spiritually and physically—into His keeping. He who owns the cattle on a thousand hills will never let us fail, if only we trust in Him.

THE WITCH OF ENDOR

Saul then said to his attendants,
"Find me a woman who is a medium,
so I may go and inquire of her."
"There is one in Endor," they said.

1 SAMUEL 28:7

Saul wasn't the first hypocritical politician, and he surely wasn't the last. And the witch of Endor wasn't the first woman who knew she was making a living illegally. A fine pair of duplicitous people they were.

As the Philistines massed to attack Israel, Saul asked God about his situation, but heaven seemed to have closed up to him. No response came, no matter what Saul tried. Desperate with fear, Saul took matters into his own hands.

Though he had tossed the spiritists and mediums out of Israel, Saul asked his attendants where to find one. They knew—and we have to wonder how, if they were faithful Jews. Whatever the case, once Saul knew her location, he visited to ask her to call up Samuel for him.

Either the medium wasn't so smart or her spirit was sleeping on the job, because not until she saw Samuel did she recognize Saul and his deception. But the king commanded her to proceed.

"I see a spirit coming up out of the ground," the medium reported.

"What does he look like?" asked Saul.

"An old man wearing a robe is coming up," she replied

(see 1 Samuel 28:13–14). After that incredibly definitive description, Saul was convinced it was Samuel.

Throughout his life, Saul hadn't listened much to Samuel—but suddenly, he was all ears. Explaining his situation, Saul waited for the prophet's advice.

The response could not have been worse. Samuel stated that the Lord had become Saul's enemy and was keeping a promise to take the kingdom from Saul's hands. The Philistines would win the upcoming battle, and Saul and his sons would die.

Devastated by this news—information that God had compassionately kept from him—Saul was overcome with fear to the point of physical weakness. The witch tried to get him to eat and go on his way, but it took much coaxing before he agreed to have dinner and head out. Demoralized, Saul lost the battle and his life, as predicted.

Scholars differ on their interpretation of this story. Was the image conjured up by the witch of Endor really Samuel? Perhaps not. The father of lies could have deceived the king. The awful news the apparition gave would certainly have pleased Satan. Or perhaps God permitted the prophet to give this last, damning prophecy.

Looking to the scriptures, we see that God's Word forbids all sorts of witchcraft (see Deuteronomy 18:9–12). If God wasn't upset with Saul before he visited a witch, certainly they would be at loggerheads after the appointment. A real trust in God and occult attempts to peer into the future are not good bedfellows.

Some people like to dabble in the occult—or at least

turn a blind eye to it—ignoring the dangers God warns of. This witch didn't wear a dark, pointy hat or make pets of spiders; she was more dangerous than any Halloween costume. Her craft totally demoralized the king and probably contributed to his fall.

When God does not tell us something, He has a reason for it. Don't go seeking hidden knowledge—just trust Him.

THE WOMAN ACCUSED OF ADULTERY

The teachers of the law and the Pharisees
brought in a woman caught in adultery.
They made her stand before the group and said to Jesus,
"Teacher, this woman was caught in the act of adultery."
JOHN 8:3–4

After being snatched up in the midst of an adulterous act, this woman was forced to stand before Jesus, pilloried before her accusers and the rest of the gapers around her. How painful that moment must have been! Fear, doubt, guilt, and hatred for her accusers must have flooded her aching soul.

But as far as the condemning leaders were concerned, the point of this event wasn't to bring her to justice. They wanted to corner Jesus. If He told them to stone her, as the Law of Moses commanded, He could be prosecuted for defying Roman law. If He said to let her go, He would defy God's Law. They thought they had trapped him perfectly.

But they were wrong.

One of the first clues that these men were not interested in justice was that the man with whom the woman committed adultery did not appear before Jesus. According to the law, both offenders were to be stoned. Yet only the woman stood before Jesus for judgment. Who was the man, and where had he gone?

Jesus, well aware of the craftiness of His enemies, responded perfectly. He began writing on the ground, while they threw questions at Him. Straightening up, He said, "If any one of you is without sin, let him be the first to throw a stone at her" (John 8:7). Then He returned to His writing.

Aware of their own imperfections, the older ones began to slip away; then the younger lost their nerve and followed, until no man stood before the adulteress.

"Woman," questioned Jesus, "where are they? Has no one condemned you?"

She replied, "No one, sir."

"Then neither do I condemn you," Jesus stated. "Go now and leave your life of sin" (see John 8:10–11).

Relief must have flooded this woman's soul! Not only had her accusers disappeared, Jesus had forgiven her—and given her life new direction. Perhaps at that very moment, salvation poured into her spirit. If she was wise, she never made that mistake again and began to live for her Lord instead.

We've walked in this woman's shoes, haven't we? As we've done wrong, we've worried that others might find out. Perhaps our sins might not have been "big ones" like adultery, but we've felt the fear of public opinion against us, even when no one knew what we did. Inside, we've wondered if life could ever be the same if our wrongdoing went public.

Or maybe we've had others publicly accuse us—and hated them for their venom as they announced our sins to one and all. Whatever the case, we've all experienced painful wrongs and wished we had a way out of them.

Jesus is that way out. He doesn't tell us we never sinned. He doesn't excuse us, but He takes the wrong on Himself, pays the price for it, and He commands us to live for Him. And in His power, we can do that—though not perfectly. Daily we come to Him for forgiveness, and daily we receive it.

Just like the woman caught in the act of adultery.

THE WOMAN AT THE WELL

When a Samaritan woman came to draw water,
Jesus said to her, "Will you give me a drink?". . .
The Samaritan woman said to him,
"You are a Jew and I am a Samaritan woman.
How can you ask me for a drink?"
(For Jews do not associate with Samaritans.)
JOHN 4:7–9

When this woman walked to the well, she couldn't imagine the barriers about to fall. The division between her people and Jesus' people was just the first of the walls about to disintegrate.

She was a member of a people who had been resettled in the land, moved there by the king of Assyria after he conquered Samaria in 722 BC. They had been taught and partially accepted the faith of Israel, but retained their old, pagan religions, too (see 2 Kings 17:24–41). Such syncretism was abhorrent to faithful Jews, so they avoided these Samaritans, whom they considered unclean.

Traveling from Judea to Galilee, Jesus and His followers had to pass through Samaria—unless they wanted to take a long detour. They chose the shorter road, and Jesus sat by a Samaritan well while His disciples went off to buy food.

When the woman approached the well, Jesus asked her for a drink. She responded with surprise and mockery, used to the idea that no Jew would accept water from her—any faithful Jew would have considered himself ceremonially unclean if he touched a cup she had handled.

Apparently this was a woman who had thought over spiritual things, even if she didn't have them right. So Jesus led her into a deeper discussion, mentioning the "living water" He could give her.

At first she took him literally, thinking He meant the water within the well, and deriding Him for offering her water He could not reach. Did He think He was greater than Jacob, whose well this was? Christ persisted, telling her plainly that He spoke of eternal life—but she still didn't quite catch His point. Her interest remained with Samaritan religious history, not really a vital faith.

But, intrigued at the thought of parting with her heavy water jar, she asked for Jesus' water. Since the water He spoke of was eternal life, He confronted her numerous sins. In opposition to Jewish law, this woman had had five husbands, and had not married the sixth man she then lived with. Even in today's loose culture, she might have raised a few eyebrows among those who knew her sexual history.

Perhaps in an effort to avoid Jesus' uncomfortable truth, the woman turned the discussion to His ability to know things she had never told Him—and then started a diversionary topic about the proper place to worship. Jesus answered her question, pointed her toward the spiritual nature of real worship, and declared Himself the Messiah. At some point, all the barriers of religion and nationality fell, and she believed in Jesus.

When the disciples returned, the woman took her opportunity to tell all her neighbors, even the ones who criticized her immorality. "He told me everything I ever did" (John 4:39) was her testimony. The Samaritans invited Jesus to stay for a couple of days, and in that time many were converted.

When we read this story, how do we see ourselves? Are we the wounded woman at the well, with a long history of sin behind us? If so, we can take heart in the forgiveness of the Savior, who confronts our sins, calls us to Himself, and forgives us.

Or are we the one witnessing to the lost? Like Jesus, we have heard many objections and need to cut through unimportant diversions and quickly get to the real message. Few of the people we speak to will readily accept our witness. Like Jesus, we need to patiently and lovingly deal with the important issues and turn each person's thoughts to real faith.

Either way, when the barriers fall, we will worship God "in spirit and in truth" (John 4:24).

THE WOMAN OF TEKOA

When the woman from Tekoa went to the king,
she fell with her face to the ground
to pay him honor, and she said,
"Help me, O king!"

2 SAMUEL 14:4

If we were giving an acting award to women of the Bible, it would have to go to the woman from Tekoa. With her thespian abilities, she tried to bring peace to a nation.

King David had banished his rebellious son, Absalom, but this father's heart still ached for his errant child. So Joab, David's nephew and commander of his army, called on the wise woman of Tekoa to go to the king. She asked the king's help and, following Joab's script, described a family situation very similar to that between David's sons Amnon and Absalom—one son had killed the other, she reported, and her clan demanded that the killer be put to death. The king promised to intervene.

Then she confronted David with his own family situation, for he had not brought Absalom back from banishment. "God does not take away life; instead he devises ways so that a banished person may not remain estranged from him" (2 Samuel 14:14), she reasoned, calling on the king to do likewise.

Immediately, David recognized Joab's hand in this, and the woman admitted it. The king called for Absalom's return, but he would not see his son for two years.

This nameless woman wanted to bring peace to her nation. Though the peace she sought was a long time coming—and did not last long—that wasn't her fault, because Absalom foolishly rebelled against his father.

We, too, sometimes need to seek peace in our own families and communities. Are willing to work with others to help them understand the need for forgiveness? Can we gently help them see how their own mistaken choices have led to painful situations, and give them hope for change? If so, we've become peacemakers, and God will bless us.

THE WOMAN WHO ANOINTED JESUS' FEET

Then he turned toward the woman and said to Simon,
"Do you see this woman? I came into your house.
You did not give me any water for my feet,
but she wet my feet with her tears
and wiped them with her hair.
You did not give me a kiss, but this woman,
from the time I entered, has not stopped kissing my feet.
You did not put oil on my head,
but she has poured perfume on my feet."

LUKE 7:44–46

The scene is a party at Simon the Pharisee's house. All the correct people must have been there: friends and acquaintances who prided themselves on their holy living, and maybe even a few really important men of faith. But one uninvited guest found her way in, carrying a jar of perfume. She slipped up to Jesus and, in the weeping of repentance, began to anoint His feet, first with her tears, then with the perfume.

Simon, who thought Jesus was just a prophet, immediately began to question His claims. After all, if Jesus had God's wisdom, couldn't He tell what everyone in Galilee already knew—that this woman was a terrible sinner? But before the Pharisee could speak, Jesus confronted his thoughts by telling a story of two men. They were both indebted to a moneylender—one owed five hundred denarii, about five hundred days' wages, while the other owed only fifty. Which one, Jesus questioned, would love him more when the moneylender forgave the debt?

The religious man, an able student though doubtful of Jesus' point, answered quickly that he supposed it would be the one with the bigger debt.

Jesus turned Simon's attention to the sinful woman. He gently rebuked Simon for not providing the hospitality customary to a guest: water to bathe His dusty feet. But that failure had made the way for this repentant sinner, who washed Jesus' feet with her tears and anointed them with the perfume. And she had not stopped with these signs of love, but kissed His feet, too. Because she was forgiven for many sins, Jesus told the proud religionist, she loved much. The clear implication was that since Simon's sins were so few (at least in his own eyes), he loved little.

Turning to the woman, Jesus said, "Your sins are forgiven" (Luke 7:48), causing an immediate whispering among the honorable guests. Who was this man who claimed to forgive sins? They knew only God could do that—and wondered what Jesus was claiming for Himself.

To complete the lesson, Jesus told the woman, "Your faith has saved you; go in peace" (Luke 7:50).

Scripture does not specifically say what sins this woman committed. But many scholars have concluded she was a prostitute. What an ending she brought to a very proper party! Guests probably talked about the event for days, if not weeks, and wondered about Jesus, the man who forgave her.

For Jesus, it was clear: It isn't how much faith you carry into a relationship with Him, it's how much forgiveness you receive when you place your sins at His feet.

What was true for this sinful woman is true for us, too. Are we, like Simon, sitting pridefully on our faith, thinking our own good works lead to salvation? If so, look out! Our good works are like filthy rags to our perfect Lord (see Isaiah 64:6). They will never get us to heaven.

But if, like this woman, we come to Jesus aware of the awfulness of our sins, asking Him to forgive them, our lives are made new in a way Simon, the proud Pharisee, may have never known.

Who are we like in this story? Simon and his guests? Or the forgiven woman?

THE WOMAN WHO TOUCHED JESUS' CLOAK

As Jesus was on his way, the crowds almost crushed him.
And a woman was there who had been
subject to bleeding for twelve years,
but no one could heal her.
She came up behind him and touched the edge of his cloak,
and immediately her bleeding stopped.

LUKE 8:42–44

Many women must have touched, brushed against, or otherwise had contact with Jesus' garments. But scripture records only one being healed by such a touch. The difference? Her faith told her that just a touch would lead to her healing—and it did.

For twelve years this woman had suffered from bleeding of some sort—we know no more of her medical condition, but that is enough. The emotional and physical need had ravaged her. Not only had her body endured misery, but because she had been "unclean" according to the Law, she had been an outcast spiritually, too. She could not approach the temple, no matter how deep her faith. And other Jews would have kept her at a distance, to avoid contamination. Hers must have been a lonely life. Mark 5:26 tells us she had gone to many doctors, spending all her money in her search for healing.

In a last effort, she came to Jesus. Reports had told her of His ability to heal. But this time things were different from her doctors' visits. She had nothing to offer Him but her unclean, impoverished self. No money, no importance, no hope.

Jesus was on His way to heal someone else, the daughter of a synagogue leader, when the woman touched His clothing. Poor, humble, and diseased, perhaps she thought she didn't deserve as much as a moment of the Savior's time. Or maybe she expected an outcry against her condition, for faithful Jews did all they could to avoid contact with the unclean.

As her fingers briefly latched on to the cloth, her body responded to Jesus' power. Suddenly, the bleeding stopped.

Just then, Jesus turned, asking, "Who touched me?" (Mark 5:31). Though His disciples doubted His words, pointing out that He was surrounded by a crowd, Jesus insisted someone had grasped Him with purpose. Of course, in His divinity, He must have known which person had held the cloak between her fingers—but He wanted her to come forward with her testimony.

Fearfully, perhaps thinking He would criticize her for wrongly taking advantage of Him, the woman fell at Jesus' feet. But the Lord didn't react with disgust or try to keep her at a distance. To Him, she was as important as the synagogue leader's child, and because of her need and her faith, she was deserving of His time and attention.

Then, before the entire crowd, the woman who had hoped to go unknown declared the truth of her healing.

Jesus replied mildly, "Daughter, your faith has healed you. Go in peace" (Mark 5:34).

What a thrill! What all the doctors could not accomplish, one touch of Jesus' cloak had done. Faith sprung up like a fountain in her heart as she rejoiced in her healing.

Like this woman, each of us needs Jesus' powerful touch. It may be a physical illness, or it may be spiritual. Like the woman, we desperately need healing. We come to Jesus poor and hopeless, seeking Him as the only possibility for healing.

What do you need to bring to Jesus? Approach Him with your need in both hands, and you will find Him right beside you.

ZILPAH

And Laban gave unto his daughter Leah
Zilpah his maid for an handmaid.
GENESIS 29:24 KJV

Upon her marriage, Laban gave his eldest daughter, Leah, a servant of her own. Perhaps Zilpah looked forward to this new place that would give her more importance.

But instead of happiness, a good deal of sorrow was headed her way. Jacob, Leah's husband, hadn't wanted to marry Leah. So he ended up marrying Leah's sister, Rachel, too. The sisters quickly began a battle of the babies to see who could give Jacob the most children. When Leah thought her childbearing days were over, she gave Zilpah to her husband as a concubine.

How did Zilpah feel about all this? We don't know. But we do know she felt blessed to have her first child, naming him *Gad* (meaning "good fortune" or "a troop"). It seems her outlook was positive, even though life wasn't perfect.

Zilpah obviously delighted in her children, since she named her second son *Asher*, which means "happy." But the marital relations in the camp brought a good deal of sorrow and contention, too.

And when Jacob returned to his homeland, it wasn't his beloved Rachel he put out in front of their caravan, in harm's way. It was Zilpah and Rachel's maid, Bilhah, also Jacob's concubine. These women were not loved for themselves—Jacob loved Rachel. The other three were primarily desired for the children they bore, who would start the twelve tribes of Israel.

Like Zilpah, none of us have perfect lives. But do we focus on the less than perfect or thank God for the many blessings He sends our way? We can choose to live in God's joy or in complaining. Which will make us happier?

ZIPPORAH

And Moses was content to dwell with the man:
and he gave Moses Zipporah his daughter.

EXODUS 2:21 KJV

You'd think that a powerful leader like Moses would have
married a woman strong in faith, wouldn't you? Well, you'd
be wrong.

Moses married Zipporah, the daughter of a Midianite
priest named Reuel (or Jethro). The Bible never tells us
what gods she worshiped, but it also doesn't show her as a
believer. In fact, her only action recorded in scripture is the
circumcision of one of her sons. This somewhat obscure
passage says that God, angered at Moses' disobedience, was
prepared to kill him. Zipporah concluded it was because
Moses had not circumcised one of their sons and unhappily
did the job herself.

A family disagreement on the subject—Midianite
tradition called for the rite when the child was older—
had probably caused Moses' lapse. Certainly his wife's
attitude following the circumcision was not a pleasant one,
so the issue may have been a bone of contention for some
time.

Zipporah is last mentioned, briefly, in Exodus 18:2,
when Jethro returns her and their sons to Moses. Scholars
believe Moses may have left his family in Jethro's safekeep-
ing while he made the dangerous trip to Egypt.

Zipporah did God's will only when her husband's life

was threatened—when push came to shove, so to speak. Do we do the same? Will we wait until we face serious trouble before we obey, or will we consistently obey our Lord?

If you've read this entire book, you know what the answer should be. Go live the adventure of faith!

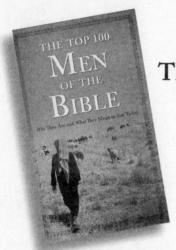